LOUIS PASTEUR

AND THE FOUNDING OF

MICROBIOLOGY

LOUIS PASTEUR

AND THE FOUNDING OF

MICROBIOLOGY

Jane Ackerman

MORGAN
REYNOLDS
Publishing, Inc.

620 South Elm Street, Suite 223
Greensboro, North Carolina 27406
http://www.morganreynolds.com

CONTENTS

Louis Pasteur in his laboratory.
(Courtesy of Musée Pasteur, Paris.)

CHAPTER ONE
A DANGEROUS DECISION

When nine-year-old Joseph Meister was bitten by what appeared to be a rabid dog on July 6, 1885, his doctor in Alsace, France, treated him the only way he knew how. He applied carbolic acid to cauterize, or burn, the flesh around the wounds. If the boy had in fact contracted rabies, it was probably too late to stop the fatal disease from entering his bloodstream and killing him. The doctor held out one hope. He knew that the famous scientist Louis Pasteur, in Paris, was experimenting on a vaccine. He advised Joseph's mother to take her son to plead with Pasteur for help.

Louis Pasteur rarely responded to interruptions of his work, but Joseph's story got his attention. He examined the boy and found fourteen bite wounds. He wrote in his notebook: "Severely bitten on the middle finger of the right hand, on the thighs, and on the leg by the same rabid dog that tore his trousers, threw him down and would have devoured him if it had not been for the arrival of a mason armed with two iron bars...."

Joseph Meister in 1885.

For five years, Pasteur had been researching rabies, a deadly disease of the central nervous system. He had developed vaccines for three other animal diseases, but rabies was proving more difficult to conquer. By the time the Meisters arrived on his doorstep, Pasteur had managed to concoct a series of injections he hoped would gradually make a person immune. He had successfully completed a test of his new method on dogs, but had tried the vaccine on a human only once—and that little girl had died. Julie-Antoinette Poughon had already begun to exhibit the symptoms of rabies when she arrived seeking treatment, however, and at that point, it was unlikely the vaccine could have helped her.

Joseph Meister's situation was further complicated because there was no way to know if he was actually infected. If Pasteur waited until he began to exhibit symptoms, it would be too late to save the boy. Rabies was always fatal; if Meister was infected, giving him the vaccine might save his life. Pasteur had no way of knowing if the vaccine was too strong, or if it might cause unforeseen side effects. The vaccine could very well be fatal, and end Pasteur's career in disgrace. His many enemies might even attempt to have him charged with murder. Even worse, the progress toward the development of life-saving vaccines would be slowed. Pasteur's decision was made more difficult when his assistant, a medical doctor, refused to participate in treating the boy, arguing the vaccine was not ready for human trials.

Pasteur was a chemist, not a medical doctor, so he sought the opinion of two doctors he trusted. After examining Joseph, they both agreed that if he was infected, he would die if not treated. Pasteur should try the vaccine—immediately.

The inoculations began that very evening, July 6, and Meister's life depended on the vaccine working faster than the rabies virus. Pasteur looked on as a physician, Dr. Grancher, stuck the needle into Joseph's skin.

He received thirteen shots over the next ten days. As each syringe injected more virulent strains of the deadly virus into the boy, Pasteur became increasingly anxious. He hovered over Joseph, watching for any signs of

Pasteur used rabbits to develop his rabies vaccine. *(Courtesy of Institut Pasteur, Paris.)*

rabies, while Joseph played happily with the other residents of the lab: rabbits, chickens, dogs, and mice. The night before Joseph's last injection, Pasteur's wife wrote to their grown children: "This will be another bad night for your father. He cannot come to terms with the idea of applying a measure of last resort to this child. And yet now he has to go through with it." On July 16, Pasteur and his associates injected into Joseph's body what would normally be a fatal dose of the rabies virus. Pasteur fretted, observing the boy as keenly as he would any important specimen. Although Joseph seemed healthy, Pasteur, haunted by visions, slept poorly. He pictured the first subtle signs of rabies appearing, then gradually consuming the boy until the final, horrible death.

But twenty-five days after the first shot, Joseph

Meister was still healthy. Pasteur gave him one of the rabbits as a pet, and Joseph kissed his "dear M. Pasteur" goodbye.

Louis Pasteur was born in the tiny French village of Dôle on December 27, 1822. He lived in a plain house tucked between run-down dwellings on a narrow street called the Rue des Tanneurs (Road of the Tanners). The family's ancestors had been shepherds, as the name Pasteur indicates.

Louis's father, Jean-Joseph, worked as a tanner. He had fought in the Napoleonic Wars and earned distinction in a battle against the Spanish. As a reward, he was named a knight of the Legion of Honor. When peace returned, Jean-Joseph Pasteur resumed tanning, determined to make a decent living for his family. He practiced a strong work ethic and taught it to young Louis. Jean-Joseph was known as a slow, careful thinker, quiet to the point of being secretive. Louis's mother, Jeanne-Étiennette, was more enthusiastic and imaginative.

Patriotism, hard work, and traditional values were deeply ingrained in the Pasteur family. Intensely patriotic, Jean-Joseph hung his sword on the tannery wall near a picture of Napoleon and, on Sundays, he would walk on the roads near Arbois, wearing his ribbon from the Legion of Honor on his wide lapels. Other walkers could see the military decoration from forty yards away.

Louis had three sisters, one older (Virginie) and two younger (Joséphine and Emilie). Before Louis's birth, another son (Jean-Denis) died when only a few months

Pasteur was born in this house, in Dôle, in the winter of 1822. *(Courtesy of Musée Pasteur, Paris.)*

old. The Pasteur family lived briefly in Marnoz, then in 1827, they moved to the village of Arbois, nestled in the Jura Mountains in southern France. Life was tough in the Jura, and the people there were fiercely loyal to each other. It was in Arbois that Emilie, age three, developed a fever that left her epileptic and mentally retarded.

The Pasteurs' simple house sat on the outskirts of Arbois alongside the Cuisance River. The strong odors from their basement and backyard tannery mingled with the fruity aroma from nearby vineyards. Louis, a stocky boy of five, ran errands for his mother and worked alongside his father. After soaking, rinsing, and scraping the animal skins, they covered the hides with dog or chicken dung. Tannin, a chemical from the bark of oak trees, turned the hide into soft, supple leather.

Louis's father taught him how to read with books about France's military glory under Napoleon. Jean-Joseph handed down war memories, turning them into lessons about honor, justice, and duty. Young Pasteur soaked up his father's patriotism.

Louis loved and admired his father, but he became engrossed in sketching and painting, activities his hard-working father considered frivolous. Louis developed into a fine painter, composing detailed portraits in his teen years that captured not only the physical likeness of his subjects, but the personality as well. His ability to accurately observe details would later serve him well in his scientific work.

Besides painting, Pasteur loved playing games:

Louis made this pastel portrait of his father in 1838. The portrait of his mother was done in 1836. *(Courtesy of Musée Pasteur, Paris.)*

marbles, capture-the-flag, swimming, and sliding on the ice on wooden shoes or a sled. Louis and his friends helped with the wine harvest, and at the banquets Louis enjoyed eating *gaudes*, cornmeal mush with fresh cream. His square forehead and gray-green eyes usually held a serious expression. His friend Jules Vercel later said: "He wasn't a rogue like the others; he re-entered his home peacefully, books and notebooks under his arm...." While they often fished from the bridge, Pasteur later told Vercel he had never liked to fish. When it came to trapping birds, Louis, who was exquisitely sensitive to suffering, adamantly refused.

When Pasteur was nine, a wolf with rabies attacked people from his village. He witnessed a farmer being held down by friends while the village blacksmith plunged a red-hot iron into the bite wound. That man survived, but eight others perished from the painful disease. For months, everyone in the village lived in terror of the rabid wolf.

School classes were held in a spare room at the town hall, where students were divided into groups and taught by monitors. Although Pasteur won some minor prizes, he generally did not excel. He worked slowly and deliberately, and his teachers, while noting his diligence and discipline, did not consider him unusually bright.

When Pasteur was fourteen, his school principal, Romanet, detected something other teachers had missed: a fertile imagination simmering beneath his disciplined intellect. Romanet took walks with Louis, and talked to the youth of attending *collège* in Paris. (A collège is similar to an American high school.)

Most sons followed in their fathers' footsteps, and

This sixteenth-century woodcut depicts men trying to overpower a rabid dog. Before Pasteur's vaccine, rabies often filled entire villages with terror.

CANIS RABIDVS.

Louis was Jean-Joseph's only surviving son. But Jean-Joseph did not mind if his son did not become a tanner; he valued education and saw teaching as a noble profession. He approved of the plan. But sending Louis to Paris was a risky proposition for a family with little money to spare, and the city could be dangerous, especially for a naïve country boy not yet sixteen. Even so, Louis's friend Jules Vercel was going. A man named Barbet, who operated a boardinghouse in Paris, was willing to take in Louis at a reduced rate in exchange for tutoring others.

On a rainy, bitterly cold October morning in 1838, Louis and Jules huddled under an awning next to the coachman. As they pulled away, Louis gazed backward at his parents, and then at the steeple in the center of Arbois. Eventually, even the outline of the Jura Mountains faded into the distance.

Compared to Arbois, Paris was crowded and dirty. Tall, grimy houses pressed in on narrow streets, shutting out the sunlight. Louis bristled at responding to drum rolls and wearing the Collège Saint Louis uniform. But most of all, he disliked Paris because it was far from home. Pasteur told Vercel, "If I could only get a whiff of the tannery yard, I feel I should be cured."

Louis lived on a cul-de-sac on the Impasse des Feuillantines, a dead end. His first foray in Paris also hit a dead end. He tried to study, but could not concentrate. He had no appetite, and would lie awake at night for hours, thinking of home and whispering the line: "How

Map of France, Pasteur's beloved homeland. Places of importance to Pasteur and his career are shown in boldface type.

endless unto watchful anguish, Night doth seem." Home-sickness merged into depression. After a long, torturous month, Louis packed up his things and returned to Arbois.

Although in familiar surroundings again, Louis remained silent. Painting seemed his only comfort, and he spent long hours capturing the smallest details of a person's face. He later enjoyed the performing arts as well, and earned a major role in a play written by Molière, the great French playwright. For years afterward, the townspeople spoke of his abilities as an actor and artist.

After a short time at his old school, Pasteur studied for two and a half years in nearby Besançon, where his father traveled several times a year to sell skins. As in Paris, Louis tutored to earn money for his room and board. He reveled in making his own money and was given his own room, which to him meant less distraction from work. He strained his already poor eyesight in the candlelight and began wearing eyeglasses for short-sightedness. Migraine headaches tormented him, especially during exams.

At Besançon, Pasteur first kept to himself, uncommunicative like his father. Eventually, he formed a deep friendship with a fellow student, Charles Chappuis. They studied together and took long walks, discussing science, literature, and Chappuis's field of study, philosophy.

When Chappuis moved on to Paris, Louis became lonely. He wrote: "You remember those days last year when I did not answer when spoken to, when I was as dull as dishwater. Today I was like that again. The only pleasure that is left to me is to receive letters… Therefore, dear friend, write to me often."

Louis wrote letters to Chappuis, and sent homework to his father and sister Joséphine so they could learn also. Knowing of his family's sacrifices, Louis offered to pay for Joséphine's schooling by taking on additional tutoring, but his father declined. Louis wrote advice to his sisters, sometimes tender, sometimes patronizing:

"...will power opens the doors to brilliant and happy careers; work allows us to pass through them, and once we have run the course, success will crown our achievement." Willpower, to him, stood for an inner strength he had previously been unable to muster. After his failure in Paris, Louis was determined not to weaken again.

Pasteur developed a close friendship with Charles Chappuis while they were students together in Besançon. Chappuis, shown here in a sketch by Pasteur, encouraged Louis to return to Paris to further his education. *(Courtesy of Institut Pasteur, Paris.)*

Pasteur also wrote home of his budding love for science: "Once one is used to working, one can no longer live without it. And of course, everything in the world depends on it; in science, one is happy; in science one rises above all others." His early experience with mathematics, on the other hand, had quite a different effect on him, and his letters expressed the lack of enthusiasm he had for the study of numbers and formulas.

Confident in his knowledge, confident in himself, Pasteur failed his first exam for a science degree at Besançon. His family's faith in him was shaken. He wrote to them, "How often have I cursed that baccalauréat in science that you seem to consider beyond me." He was faced with a decision: to give up his studies or to reapply himself toward the next year's exams.

Louis wanted to join Chappuis in Paris and continue his studies there, but Jean-Joseph objected to this course. Pasteur, unhappily, remained in Besançon. Chappuis wrote: "…I advised you to go to Paris; each time your father created some obstacle! But do what he wishes, and never forget that it is perhaps because he loves you too much that he never does what you ask."

After a year of studying, Pasteur took his exams a second time, which he described as "a hundred times more difficult." He received several high scores. But the future chemist received a chemistry grade of "mediocre." This was a huge blow, forcing Louis to doubt the two years he had devoted to study. He knew he could master the material and was deeply embarrassed by his test scores.

He applied to the École Normale Supérieure, the legendary collège in Paris, where the most prestigious teachers taught the most promising students. Louis fought migraines during the entire six-hour entrance exam. He passed, ranked fifteenth of the twenty-two students accepted. He had been working towards this opportunity for years but was so disappointed in his performance, he refused the invitation. He would not be "mediocre" again. Louis set his will toward another year of studying in order to retake the entrance exam.

Defying his father's wishes, Louis went to Paris to prepare. Just before leaving, he painted one last portrait, a pastel of his father, as if to imprint the image in his mind. He returned to the Collège Saint Louis, and again tutored to help pay his way. Money was tight, and his father criticized his spending. After reminding his father that he paid for his own courses, he accounted for his other expenses: candles, heating wood, a tablecloth to cover the cracks, pens, ink, paper, and a book on physics by Benjamin Franklin. He prepared long hours for the entrance exam. His only distraction was his friend. He wrote to his parents, "Whom do I frequent here? Chappuis. And whom else? Chappuis."

Pasteur's father worried that his son, living

Jean-Baptiste Dumas's lectures at the Sorbonne profoundly influenced Pasteur's decision to study chemistry.

in the Latin Quarter of Paris, would fall in with bad company. Louis wrote back: "When one wishes to keep straight, one can do so in this place as well as in any other; it is those who have no strength of will that succumb."

Strength of will became Louis Pasteur's most defining characteristic. He was awakened each morning at 5:30 a.m. by the night watchman with the words, "Come! Drive out the demon of laziness!" His physics instructor gave him extra problems to solve. He often spent his free time in the library, reading scientific journals and biographies of great scientists. He immersed himself completely in work.

In 1843, at age twenty, Louis passed the École Normale entrance exam once again, this time ranking fourth and earning high honors. While waiting for the school year to begin, a proud Louis roamed Paris. At the nearby Sorbonne, another superb university, Pasteur attended speeches by the famous chemist, Jean-Baptiste Dumas. Large crowds filled the auditorium when Dumas spoke. He gave clear, eloquent talks that showcased the elegance of his subject. Pasteur was so enthralled by Dumas's lectures, by his fame and powerful presence, that he decided to devote himself to the science of chemistry.

CHAPTER TWO
EMERGING SCIENTIST

At the École Normale, Pasteur combined twelve hours of studying each day with extra laboratory work. His father, who would have been satisfied with Louis achieving a modest teaching position, wrote: "You work immoderately...It isn't good to be always high-strung. Ruining your health is not the way to success!" Louis's father encouraged him to pursue mathematics as those teachers were paid well and worked comfortable hours. But Pasteur had already set himself on chemistry and three years later had his degree. During his schooling, Pasteur did not always rank first on his exams, but his friend Chappuis was fond of saying: "You will see what Pasteur will be."

His academic work completed, Pasteur wrote to the famous chemist Dumas, whose speeches had so mes-

The legendary École Normale Supérieure, in Paris.

merized him, pleading for a job with his laboratory staff. Dumas, a pioneer of organic chemistry, had more than enough eager young assistants, and turned him down. Pasteur was on the verge of leaving Paris for a teaching position in a rural town when one of his former teachers intervened. Antoine Jerôme Balard, discoverer of the element bromine, saw potential in Pasteur and hired him to work in a lab alongside the famous chemist, Auguste Laurent, whose experiments advanced our understanding of organic compounds.

Pasteur gravitated towards big scientific problems that dealt with the "infinitely small." He first focused on crystals—solid forms with regular geometric shapes—reading everything he could find on the subject. Chemists wanted to know if crystals could tell them anything about their component parts: tiny invisible particles we call atoms and molecules. Using an instrument called a polarimeter, Pasteur studied how rays of light bend when they go through a solution of crystals. He was intrigued by a contradictory finding that had stumped top scientists. Eilhardt Mitscherlich, an eminent German chemist, had noticed that a particular crystal (tartaric acid) bent light, and that a second crystal (paratartaric, also called racemic, acid) had the same chemical formula but did not bend light.

Pasteur proposed that the different effect the crystals had on light was related to their symmetry. Perhaps, though the two crystals had the same chemical makeup, one crystal was symmetrical and the other was not. Pasteur carefully

Tartaric acid crystal, as seen through a microscope. (© Sinclair Stammers/Photo Researchers, Inc.)

measured the minute sides and angles of the crystals and found that tartaric acid crystals, which bent light to the right, were indeed asymmetrical on the right side. This made sense to him. He then examined paratartaric acid crystals, expecting to find them symmetrical. Pasteur reported his excitement at his discovery: "For an instant my heart stopped beating: all the crystals exhibited the facets of asymmetry!"

This discovery was exciting but only served to complicate the question. Now Pasteur needed to understand how some asymmetrical crystals could bend light while others did not. Upon closer examination of paratartaric acid crystals, he discovered there were two kinds of particles with two kinds of asymmetry: right-handed and left-handed, also known as mirror-image particles.

With painstaking care, Pasteur used a fine-pointed needle to separate the paratartaric acid crystals into right-handed and left-handed particles. Just as he had hoped, the right-handed ones bent light to the right, and the left-handed ones bent light to the left. Now came the critical test. He measured out equal weights of the right- and left-handed crystals and combined them in solution.

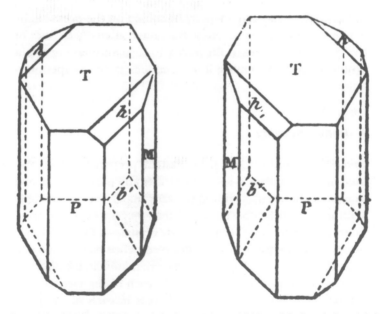

Pasteur's drawing of asymmetrical crystals, exhibiting right-handed and left-handed asymmetry. Note that the crystal on the right is a mirror image of the crystal on the left. *(Courtesy of Institut Pasteur, Paris.)*

When placed in the polarimeter, the light did not bend; the crystals cancelled each other out.

Pasteur rushed from the lab and grabbed another instructor, dragging him to the Luxembourg Gardens to gush of his discovery. Balard broadcast the news. Many scientists were skeptical, though, including Jean-Baptiste Biot, a leading expert in crystallography and the inventor of the polarimeter used by Pasteur. He offered the use of his own laboratory and ma-

At first skeptical, Jean-Baptiste Biot was thrilled by Pasteur's realization of asymmetrical crystals and their effect on light. *(Courtesy of Institut Pasteur, Paris.)*

terials so Pasteur could prepare all the crystals under Biot's watchful eyes.

Since right-handed crystals are common in nature and were known to bend light to the right, Biot chose to start with the left. If left-handed crystals bent light to the left, he could jump to the logical conclusion that the two combined would cancel each other out. Biot himself passed light through the crystals with the polarimeter. The light deviated so strongly to the left that measurement was unnecessary. Biot seized Pasteur's arm and said, "My dear boy, I have loved science so much all my life that this stirs my heart."

The discovery of molecular asymmetry launched Pasteur's career and initiated an entirely new field: stereochemistry, the study of the ways molecules are arranged in space, and how that arrangement affects their function. Biot became a mentor, and supported Pasteur when he presented papers to the renowned Academy of Sciences. Pasteur had a tendency to make grandiose pronouncements about the importance of his own work and Biot cautioned him against doing so, as such boastfulness might harm his reputation and career. When others criticized Pasteur, Biot provided moral support, advising the young man that, often, the best work has the most vocal critics. Pasteur dedicated many of his papers to Biot, and the two developed a deep, lifelong friendship.

This sketch of Louis Pasteur is based on a photograph taken in 1846. *(Courtesy of Musée Pasteur, Paris.)*

In 1848, while Pasteur was holed up in

FEBRUARY REVOLUTION, 1848

King Louis-Philippe had taken the throne following a revolution in 1830. The legislature elected him and he was known as the "citizen king," a people's monarch. He at first ruled as a moderate, but began to impose more repressive measures after rebellions and threatened assassinations. Economic recession in 1846-47 further weakened his support among the people.

His rule became ever harsher until finally the popular tide broke against him. Thousands rushed into the streets during the February Revolution of 1848, demanding a new Republic and expanded voting rights. Louis-Philippe went into exile in England. Louis-Napoléon, nephew of Napoleon Bonaparte, called on his famous uncle's name to win popular election as president of the Second Republic. He would later stage a coup, and dub himself Napoleon III, emperor of the Second Empire.

his laboratory, a revolution began in the streets of Paris. There were executions, revolutionary plots, and riots. Pasteur had once petitioned to be exempted from military service. But his father had instilled in him a sense of national pride and duty and, now, his patriotism flared in the midst of revolution. He donated all of his savings and joined the National Guard. Even so, Pasteur's work was not derailed by politics. He spent as much time as possible in his lab, more concerned with the view through his microscope than with the view out his window.

Pasteur's parents tried to understand his dedication to science. They wrote letters expressing their happiness at the pleasure he took in his work and also of their concerns for his health and safety. He worked so hard and, in Paris, he was far from their loving care.

In May 1848, a few days after Pasteur reported his findings on crystals to the Academy of Sciences, he heard that his mother had suffered a stroke. He set out immediately, but she died just before he arrived at Arbois. His father blamed her death on the stress of Louis being exposed to danger in Paris. Louis was inconsolable. He stayed with his family for several weeks, unable to work.

Later that year, twenty-six-year-old Pasteur took his first teaching appointment as a professor of physics at the *lycée*, or high school, in Dijon. Teaching kept him busy, and he soon began to mourn his lack of time and money for research. Fortuitously, after only two months in Dijon, he was invited to substitute for a professor of chemistry at the University of Strasbourg. Pasteur left Dijon at once, not even waiting for his replacement.

In Strasbourg, he missed both his family and Chappuis. He moved in with a school chum from Besançon, Pierre Bertin, whose wit and lively manner nicely counterbalanced Pasteur's sober attitude. The only known photograph of Pasteur smiling was taken with this friend.

Pasteur was invited to dinner at the home of the university's rector, Charles Laurent (no relation to the famous chemist). Pasteur was smitten with the rector's daughter, Marie. Her warmth and enthusiasm reminded Louis of his mother and, only two weeks after their meeting, he knew that he wanted to spend his life with her.

In Pasteur's time, courting was still quite formal, with

parents initiating any discussion about marriage, and direct expression of affection considered a sign of poor upbringing. For the most part, Louis acted appropriately, breaking with tradition only once. Pasteur did not ask his father to open negotiations—he wrote to Marie's father on his own. He described his family, his modest financial situation, and his career, declaring his only assets as "good health, an honest heart, and my position at the university."

Marie's father was slow to respond. He considered young Pasteur a bit impudent. While Laurent made inquiries as to the boy's character, days stretched into weeks with no reply. Louis's uneasiness grew. He decided to approach Marie's mother, who seemed more favorably disposed to him. He wrote: "I am afraid that Mlle. Marie may be influenced by early impressions, unfavourable to me. There is nothing in me to attract a young girl's fancy. But my recollections tell me that those who have known me very well have loved me very much."

Once Marie's parents had given Pasteur permission to address her directly, he wrote in a letter delivered by her mother: "All that I beg of you, Mademoiselle, is that you will not judge me too hastily, and therefore misjudge me. Time will show you that below my cold, shy and unpleasing exterior, there is a heart full of affection for you!"

Louis and Marie spent time together, always in the presence of her parents. After she squeezed his hand one day, Pasteur's hopes soared. He wrote to her, "I woke up every morning with the thought that you wouldn't return my love, and then I wept! My work means nothing to me—to me, who was so devoted to my crystals that when I went to bed I wished the night was not so long, so that I could get back to work quicker!"

Marie's father finally accepted Pasteur's proposal. Louis's twenty-five-year-old sister, Joséphine, who had planned to keep house for Louis if he did not marry, came to Strasbourg to help him until the wedding. On May 29, 1849, three months after they first met, Louis and Marie were married. Legend has it that on the morning of the ceremony he was in the lab, immersed in his beloved crystals, and needed reminding to go to the Church of Sainte Madeleine to be wed.

Marie seemed an ideal companion for Pasteur. Kind, devoted, and cheerful, she had good judgment and common sense. She supported his ideas, took dictation, and accepted full responsibility for running the household. Pasteur's lab work took priority over his time at home, sometimes to Marie's dismay. Louis confided to Chappuis: "I am often scolded by Madame Pasteur, but I make her feel better by telling her that I am leading her into posterity."

Marie put up with Pasteur's eccentricities, including his tendency to work too much and neglect his family. In their early years together, Pasteur poured money into his work that might have otherwise allowed the family more material comforts. He did not earn very much

Marie Pasteur, several years after she and Louis were married. *(Courtesy of Musée Pasteur, Paris.)*

money, but never hesitated to buy the laboratory equipment he needed to conduct his experiments. While other wives might have been irked by Pasteur's absorption in his work, Marie came to share his passion for experimental science. Émile Roux, who worked with Pasteur for twenty years, later described her faith in him with great respect. He, along with many others who worked with the scientist, witnessed Marie's love for her husband evolve into a great enthusiasm for his studies. She not only took dictation for Louis, she took real interest in his experiments and frequently asked him to explain his work with crystals and viruses, knowing that talking about his ideas would help them gain even more clarity. As Roux recalled, Marie Pasteur was not only a loving companion to Louis, she became one of his greatest supporters and collaborators.

Marie's patience was legendary as well. Pasteur's son-in-law later recalled a time Marie wanted to attend a parade held in honor of a visit by Louis Napoleon. Pasteur had promised he would go after he finished some work at his laboratory, but the few items he planned to address turned into a full day's work. Pasteur did not return home until the parade had passed, explaining that he could not interrupt his experiments. When asked how she accommodated her husband's work habits, Marie responded that she simply never made plans.

Louis and Marie's first daughter, Jeanne, was born in Strasbourg in April 1850, and this event was followed closely by the death of Pasteur's sister Joséphine, in

September, from tuberculosis. A little more than a year later, in November 1851, the Pasteurs' only son, Jean-Baptiste, was born. Like his own father, Louis was both an authoritarian and loving husband and father.

Still seeking to understand symmetry and asymmetry, Louis traveled in 1852 to Germany, Austria, and Italy in search of clues to the mysterious formation of paratartaric acid. He enjoyed the hospitality of some scientists, who were generous with their knowledge, and experienced the deception of others who preferred to keep their work secret. His letters home to Marie often ended with: "My love to you and science forever."

Apparently, though, he did not often write to his father while on this trip. Jean-Joseph Pasteur began to feel quite isolated after the deaths of Louis's mother and Joséphine, and the marriage of Virginie. At the same time, the geographic and intellectual distance between father and son was growing larger. Initially proud of his son's honors, Jean-Joseph started feeling abandoned and resentful.

After returning from his trip, Louis wrote to his father, explaining he had not intended to make his father anxious by not writing:

> I understand you all the better because I was made, or rather because you have made me, in your image. There are days when you are bored, when you get upset by the annoyances that are part of life. Well, I am like that too!...You are too skeptical. That is a bad thing. For my age, I am already very skeptical, and I

am afraid that when I get to yours, I will surpass my model.

Pasteur expressed his hope that his success in the laboratory might make his father both happy and proud. Louis never stopped trying to please his father, though he insisted on going about it in his own way.

While most scientists thought it impossible, Pasteur eventually figured out how to convert tartaric into paratartaric acid. In November 1853, he was named to the Legion of Honor and won the prize of the Society of Pharmacy for his work with these crystals. He was not yet thirty.

For the next few years Pasteur continued tinkering with molecular symmetry, trying to produce an asymmetrical molecule by applying asymmetrical forces such as magnetism and electricity. He did not succeed, but in his attempts he determined how a molecule's spatial organization (right- or left-handedness) interacts or connects with other molecules, a critical concept in modern biology. Current research and medical applications involving hormones, enzymes, vitamins, and antibodies are all based on work the young Pasteur began in those years, but it was another type of microscopic particle that would make him famous in his own lifetime.

CHAPTER THREE
FERMENTATION

Late in 1854, Pasteur moved his young family to Lille, then the fifth largest city in France. At age thirty-two, he was made not only professor of chemistry, but dean of a new Faculty of Sciences. The University of Lille was seeking a first-rate scientist who could help the local industries, especially those producing alcohol from beet juice. The making of paint, perfume, and vinegar depended on this alcohol. When a student's father asked Louis to figure out what made his vats of beet juice spoil instead of ferment into alcohol, Pasteur was eager to prove himself.

Pasteur visited a number of beet juice factories. He talked with workers, took samples, and examined foam from the tops of the vats. Using methods native to chemistry along with the biologist's traditional instrument, the microscope, Pasteur found an answer.

In vats producing good alcohol, Pasteur found tiny, round fungi called yeast. He had never seen them before, but knew of theories suggesting they played a role in fermentation. In the spoiled vats, he found peculiar masses of foam. When he looked at that foam under his microscope, he saw countless, tiny, rod-shaped microbes tangled together. These miniature organisms had conquered the yeast and made sour lactic acid instead of alcohol.

Pasteur suggested determining which microbes were in the vats as early as possible. Then factories could discard vats with lactic microbes and select healthy yeast to start new fermentations. Pasteur, who used science to save the alcohol industry, was hailed as a hero. He said: "There is no such thing as a special category of science called applied science; there is science and there are its applications, which are related to one another as the fruit is related to the tree that has borne it."

Based on his beet-juice research, Pasteur concluded that each fermentation has its own "ferment," a particular microbe, which causes the process to occur. However, Justus von Liebig, a highly respected scientist, contended that fermentation was not a biological process, caused by microbes, but a purely chemical one, caused by a chain of reactions. Because of this, few people supported Pasteur's stance. They questioned his focus on biology. Pasteur tried to get Liebig to acknowledge the role of microbes, and even visited the older man in

Pasteur using a microscope in his laboratory. *(Courtesy of Institut Pasteur, Paris.)*

Munich. Liebig, while courteous, refused to discuss the issue. Time would show that Pasteur and Liebig were both right. Microbes are necessary for fermentation, but act through their chemical enzymes. Pasteur's work on beet juice led him to study fermentation further.

Pasteur's experiments convinced him that microorganisms caused fermentation, and his research into these tiny creatures, invisible to the naked eye, would solidify his belief in germ theory. Germ theory comes from the word germinate, which means to grow. Seeds were called germs because of their ability to produce a larger plant. People had long suspected that if plants grew from tiny seeds, so too could animals and diseases. Germ theory would not become popular or respected for some time, until equipment improved and scientists of Pasteur's era began to actually see these microorganisms.

In a remarkable paper on lactic acid fermentation presented to the scientific community at Lille, Pasteur made an extremely strong case for the biological theory of fermentation. The Academy of Sciences in Paris awarded Pasteur the prize for experimental physiology for his work on fermentation, but not all scientists appreciated his new ideas. Some laughed at the idea of tiny plants making gas (carbon dioxide), and excreting a liquid waste product (a type of alcohol). Pasteur's manner of presenting his ideas did not make them any easier to accept. Despite his growing skills as a writer and speaker, he often expressed himself in a manner that teetered between confidence and arrogance.

While Pasteur would sometimes attend a social event to advance his career, he hated taking time away from the lab and would often decline invitations or simply forget to go. He hosted the receptions required of him as dean, but when Marie was not home, he would often forget to eat dinner. In a letter to Chappuis, he repeated an expression of his mentor Jean-Baptiste Biot: "Let us all work; it is the only fun there is."

Pasteur was first nominated to the Academy of Sciences in 1857, going up against Gabriel Delafosse, one of his École Normale professors and thirty years his senior. The Academy selected Delafosse over Pasteur and, even though he knew his youth was to blame, Pasteur felt insulted. Back in Lille, he said to Marie: "I will work off the rage in my heart. How happy I'll be when I go back to read them a fine paper, crying out to myself: 'Idiots that you are, go ahead and try to do this yourselves!'"

Soon after this rebuff, Pasteur was offered the prestigious position of administrator and director of scientific studies at the École Normale. He eagerly returned to Paris, the scientific hub of France, and to his old school. Marie and their youngest, Cécile, moved with him, while Jeanne and Jean-Baptiste attended a boarding school in the Jura Mountains near their grandfather.

Three of the Pasteur's five children. Only Marie-Louise (left) and Jean-Baptiste (right) would live into adulthood. Cécile (middle) died of typhoid fever when she was twelve years old, causing Louis much grief. *(Courtesy of Musée Pasteur, Paris.)*

Today, most professors of his stature would be given a well-equipped laboratory, but then, working conditions for scientists were poor. Pasteur had to buy or make his own equipment, and he had no assistants. The only lab space he could find was in the school's attic. Five flights up, the attic consisted of two rat-infested nooks, with no space for an incubator (a warmer for culturing, or growing, microbes). Pasteur later installed one in a closet with kneeling room only, accessed by a ladder. In the summer, the attic's temperature reached ninety-seven degrees Fahrenheit, making work virtually impossible. Despite his imperfect workplace, Pasteur was happy with his burgeoning career.

In July 1858, the birth of Marie-Louise added another member to the Pasteur household. One year later, in September 1859, their eldest girl, nine-year-old Jeanne, died of typhoid fever. To his father, he wrote: "I cannot keep my thoughts from my poor little girl, so good, so happy in her little life who, in this fatal year now ending, was taken away from us."

Pasteur's description of her burial reflects the emotional trauma he experienced at her death: "I heard the sound of the coffin and of the cords that took it down to the bottom of her grave, and the sound of the earth falling on that wood, both so empty and so full...What are those letters from strangers, from friends, even family? Vain talk—drops of water taken from the fury of the ocean." Deep in despair, Pasteur was nearly inconsolable, yet young Jeanne's death refocused Pasteur's determination to understand the causes of disease.

CHAPTER FOUR
PASTEURIZATION

Up to this point, most doctors believed that disease arose spontaneously within the body, but Pasteur suspected that illness was spawned by microbes. He needed a way to prove the existence and source of what he called "these mysterious agents, so feeble in appearance yet so powerful in reality."

Scientists and philosophers had argued for centuries about whether living organisms could come from non-living substances, an idea called spontaneous generation. Before the 1700s, people believed that wasps and beetles were formed out of dung; mice and frogs from riverbanks, swamps, or slime; and maggots and flies from rotting meat. More scientific approaches were applied to the question of spontaneous generation in the 1700s. By the 1800s, animal reproduction was under-

Diagram from Pasteur's article on spontaneous generation. His research led him to conclude that disease and decay do not arise of their own accord, spontaneously, but are instead caused by microorganisms. *(Courtesy of the Library of Congress.)*

stood, but the origin of disease was still in question.

Despite warnings from Biot and Dumas that it would be a waste of time to focus on a question so seemingly impossible to answer, Pasteur forged ahead. He wrote to his old friend Chappuis in January 1860: "I hope to make soon a decisive step by solving, without the least confusion, the celebrated question of spontaneous generation…it will require nothing less than the cogency of arithmetical demonstration to convince my adversaries of my conclusions. I intend to accomplish even that."

Pasteur set up an experiment to test whether microbes generated spontaneously or were instead carried by dust in the air. He filled two flasks with yeast water, then heated them until boiling, killing any germs inside. He sealed the flasks tightly so no air could enter. He kept one flask intact and broke open the other flask so dust could enter. Soon microbes were growing, but only in the broken flask. Pasteur concluded that germs had entered on particles of dust. Thus, microbes did not grow spontaneously, but reproduced like other living things.

There were many scientists who doubted Pasteur's work, arguing that the sealed flask did not develop microbes because no oxygen was allowed to enter. Oxygen was thought to contain a life force required for spontaneous generation. Pasteur silenced those critics by repeating the experiment with swan-necked flasks, bottles with bends in the necks. The shape of the necks allowed air to enter, but gravity caused the dust in the air to settle

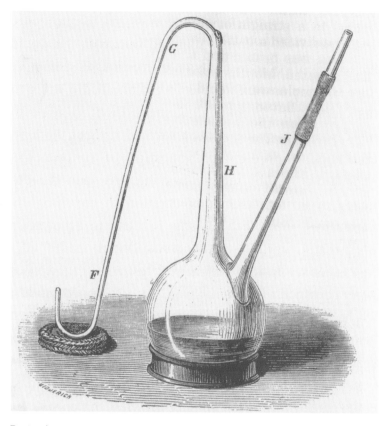

Pasteur's swan-necked flask allowed air in but kept dust particles out, helping him prove that microbes did not develop out of thin air but were carried on dust particles. *(Courtesy of Institut Pasteur, Paris.)*

in the curve of the neck, where it was trapped. The yeast water solution did not produce microbes until a bottle was tipped, allowing dust from the bend of the neck to enter the fluid.

In 1862, in a public lecture at the Sorbonne, Pasteur shone a beam of light into the dark auditorium, illuminating millions of dust particles floating in the air. Pale-faced, eyes shining through his glasses, he said:

I have taken my drop of water...full of elements most suited to the development of small beings. And I wait, I observe, I question it, I beg it to be so kind as to begin over again just to please me, the primitive act of creation; it would be so fair a sight! But it is mute!...Ah! That is because I...have kept from it the germs that float in the air; I have kept it from life, for life is a germ and a germ is life. Never will the belief in spontaneous generation arise from the mortal blow that this simple experiment has given it.

The audience, which included Princess Mathilde, novelist and playwright Alexander Dumas, writer George Sand, and other great minds of the day, gave him a standing ovation. The still unbroken flask used in his famous experiment can be seen today in the Pasteur Institute's museum.

Spontaneous generation had created intense debates, fueled by religious and political issues. Some viewed spontaneous generation as an atheistic belief, as it implied no need for a creator. The germ theory of creation implied all life came from a source, and so Pasteur was seen as a defender of religion and divine creation. Passionate and fierce, he replied:

This is not a matter of religion, philosophy, atheism, materialism, or spiritualism...It is a question of fact; I took it up without preconceived ideas, and if experiment convinced me that way I was as ready to maintain the existence of spontaneous generation as I am now persuaded that those who affirm it are blindfolded.

Felix-Archimede Pouchet was France's most prominent proponent of spontaneous generation. A highly respected naturalist, Pouchet published "Heterogenie," a controversial article that was applauded by many intellectuals, but disputed by many others, including the strongly Catholic royal family.

Pouchet did not believe dust in the air to be the source of so many germs, and wrote: "In that case, the air in which we live would almost have the density of iron." Pasteur responded that the density of germs varied with the amount of dust in the air. He set out to show that samples from places with more dust caused more growth of microbes than places with very little dust. He collected samples of air from cellars, courtyards, fields, and mountains by briefly opening sterile flasks of boiled yeast water, then quickly sealing them again. Passersby gave him strange looks as he toted his flasks down city streets and up mountainsides dressed in a black suit and tie.

As Pasteur expected, more microbes grew in flasks with air collected from dusty locales. Every flask from a Paris courtyard grew microbes, and eight of twenty from the country grew microbes. However, only one in twenty from the Alps, on the Montanvert glacier near the Mer-de-Glace, showed growth.

The scene was set for a highly publicized experimental duel, and Pouchet went to great lengths to prove Pasteur wrong. He collected samples at sea and at even higher altitudes than Pasteur, risking his life on treach-

GERM THEORY

M. T. Varro (116-27 B.C.), a Roman, was one of the first to postulate that diseases had a physical cause. He believed tiny insects found in swampy areas could enter the body and make one ill. Over the next 2000 years, as equipment improved and knowledge increased, scientists isolated and identified the bacteria responsible for most diseases.

Over the centuries, different cultures have tried to find ways to explain the existence of disease. Some people believed that disease was a punishment from their god or the work of the devil. In many places, people suspected of being witches were burned alive because they were believed to deliberately make others sick. When scientists insisted disease was the result of invisible particles in the bloodstream, people considered that explanation just as far-fetched as these other theories seem to us today.

In addition to misconceptions about what caused disease, people were at a loss for cures. Attempts included bloodletting, using leeches or scalpels; the application of innumerable herbs or poultices; and the ingestion of potions and gases. While many of these methods have been discredited by modern science, others have stood the test of time. For instance, in parts of Africa and Asia, people practiced a form of vaccination by scratching the skin of a healthy person and then applying to the scratch a few drops of an infected person's blood. As well, many of the herbs used in older medical traditions have had their healing properties confirmed.

erous mountain trails in the Pyrenees. But instead of yeast water as a medium, he used a boiled hay solution. His flasks always grew microbes. Neither Pouchet nor Pasteur yet knew that hay contained spores that survived the heating process. Pouchet mistakenly thought the

Marie holding Camille, the Pasteurs' fifth child. Like two of her siblings, Camille would succumb to fatal illness in childhood. *(Courtesy of Musée Pasteur, Paris.)*

Pasteur sometimes played croquet with his family after lunch. On rainy days he played an intense game of billiards, refusing to lose. Bertin was a regular visitor, and he and Pasteur's son, Jean-Baptiste, brought wit and hilarity into the otherwise serious household. Moments of relaxation were not always easy to come by. Pasteur's nephew, Adrien Loir, often had to sound a gong several times to lure Pasteur out of the lab for their occasional walks to the source of the Cuisance River, where they picnicked on the grass. After a short break, Pasteur would herd his assistants back to work.

In his effort to understand spoilage, Pasteur studied both local wines and the most famous wines of France. Using his microscope, Pasteur found that there were several different microbes, and that each caused a different problem. Soon he was astonishing winemakers by predicting whether a wine would taste bitter, acidic, or sour simply by looking through his microscope.

Pasteur's work was gaining him a reputation, but many winemakers were suspicious of the city scientist and his mysterious instruments. While farmers today understand the relationship between science and agriculture, Pasteur faced resistance. He calculated that *Mycoderma aceti,* the bacteria that causes wine to turn to vinegar, consumed two thousand times its own weight. Realizing that a microbe's power could be so out of proportion to its size, Pasteur recognized the immense role that tiny organisms, invisible to the naked eye, played in the earth's economy. Pasteur helped to reveal that microscopic creatures could have extraordinary capacity for destruction.

Extending his work to other substances such as milk and butter, which also spoiled, Pasteur discovered that different kinds of microbes thrive in different conditions. While studying spoiled butter, Pasteur happened to notice that microbes along the edges of the butter slides, where they were exposed to air, died. (A slide consists of two thin pieces of glass with a sample of a given substance between them.) But microbes in the middle of the slides, away from the oxygen, survived.

The idea that an organism could live without oxygen was so revolutionary that he didn't announce his discovery right away. After all, Antoine Lavoisier, the great French scientist and master of the experimental method, had proclaimed that life was impossible without atmo-

Pas
anc

his

Paste
that (
made
others
ferme
This ill
a drop
nified
times. 1
microb
necess
fermen
long, th
are t
respons
age. *(Co
Pasteur,*

from growing in wine. Methods then in use for preserving wine included adding resin, sugar, vinegar, pieces of meat, or alcohol itself. After multitudes of failed experiments, including the introduction of antiseptics, Pasteur finally discovered that heating the wine to between sixty and one hundred degrees centigrade (140 and 212 degrees Fahrenheit) for a few moments without air killed the microorganisms that caused spoilage. At long last, he had found a reliable method for preserving wine.

Many winemakers feared that heating wine would harm the taste. Pasteur invited wine-tasting experts to try both heated and unheated wines. To show that imagination and other factors can influence judgment, he used a bit of trickery. He gave two samples to the tasters—from the same bottle. Every expert claimed to taste a difference between the two, but when given the real samples, nine out of ten experts were unable to detect any differences between the heated and the unheated wines.

To test how well heating preserved wine, Pasteur arranged for ships sailing on long voyages to carry both heated and unheated wines. When they returned to port, the unheated wines had spoiled, whereas the heated wines were in excellent condition. Stored in sterile containers, heated wines remained good for several months. France could now export wines all over the world.

Pasteur's method of heating wine soon spread to

other European countries and across the Atlantic and, before long, the same process was applied to beer and milk. Disease caused by spoiled milk was virtually eliminated—a huge breakthrough in public health. The heating process was named pasteurization and is still used today with milk, wine, beer, juices, and other foodstuffs.

Pasteurization had its critics. Some complained that Pasteur took full credit for the discovery without acknowledging those who had contributed to it. Pasteur's idea to heat wine was not original—a man named Nicholas Appert had pioneered the use of heating as a method of preserving food. Pasteur defended himself vigorously, saying he had no knowledge of Appert's work and that, even if he had, it was Pasteur who first understood why heating worked.

Pasteur took out a patent to defend his establishment of the heating method to prevent spoilage and also designed equipment to carry out this heating process on a large scale at a low cost. He then gave up becoming a wealthy man; for the good of his country, he allowed his patent to go into the public domain where it could benefit the greatest number of people.

CHAPTER FIVE
SAVING SILKWORMS

The French government was not about to let Pasteur's talents go to waste. His next project was to save the French silk industry from ruin. Silk comes from the cocoons of a certain kind of caterpillar, or silkworm. The silk industry breeds millions of caterpillars and harvests their cocoons to make into fiber and sell. Silkworms eat only the leaves of mulberry trees, nicknamed the tree of gold.

Beginning in 1845, silkworm breeders began to find black spots on their worms and, soon after, the worms started dying in great numbers. The illness, called *pébrine* from the French word for pepper, spread rapidly, destroying whole harvests and farms. In 1865 alone, France lost more than eleven million dollars, ninety-seven percent of what the silk industry typically brought in.

Louis Pasteur in 1857. *(Courtesy of Musée Pasteur, Paris.)*

Dumas, Pasteur's revered teacher and friend, now a senator, pleaded with him to help. Pasteur replied that he knew absolutely nothing about silkworms. Dumas persisted, saying: "Misery is greater here than anything one can imagine."

Pasteur again insisted that he was ignorant on the subject. He had no training as a biologist or physiologist, and he had never laid eyes upon a silkworm. "So much the better," Dumas said. "For ideas, then, you will have only those that you develop as a result of your own observations."

After reading up on silkworm diseases, Pasteur saw

the wisdom in Dumas's words. No one had a clear understanding of the disease plaguing the silkworms. Attempted cures included dosing the caterpillars with wine, tar vapors, chlorine gas, sulfur, charcoal powder, and other substances.

This problem intrigued Pasteur because of its importance to France, but also because it would bring him closer to comprehending how disease spread in humans. It bothered him that so far none of his discoveries had dramatically saved lives. He traveled to Alès, in southern France near the Mediterranean, and learned about the silkworms' life cycle and breeding conditions.

Pasteur began his studies in a silkworm nursery, and was confronted almost immediately with an enigma. Some of the healthiest broods of silkworms were crawling with corpuscles (microscopic particles), while other diseased broods contained few or none. He also made an early mistake. Because he found the corpuscles later in the worms' lifecycle, he believed they were a symptom of the disease, not the cause.

In June of 1865, after only nine days in Alès, Pasteur received a telegram that his father was severely ill. Pasteur feared that, as with his mother and his daughter Jeanne, his father would die before he could reach him. Pasteur's fears were confirmed when his train was met in Arbois by his relatives, already dressed in black. That evening Pasteur wrote to Marie and their children, expressing his sorrow at his father's death and his wish to have embraced him one final time. Pasteur thanked his

LE CHOLÉRA

Cholera was one of the highly infectious diseases that Pasteur hoped to conquer. Hundreds of people died each day during the 1865 outbreak in Paris.

father for his affection and for passing on his strong work ethic, and hoped that his scientific achievements had made his father happy and proud.

Pasteur returned to Alès right away, knowing that many livelihoods depended on his progress. Just a few months later, Pasteur's youngest, two-year-old Camille, became seriously ill. By day Pasteur worked in his laboratory, and by night he watched Camille waste away. Apparently she suffered from cancer. Only a few months after his father's death, Pasteur buried Camille in Arbois, next to his mother, father, and Jeanne.

He wrote to Dumas: "My poor child died this morning; she was so lucid to the very end that when her little hands were getting cold, she constantly asked to place them into mine...."

Within a month of Camille's death, a cholera outbreak began in Paris, killing hundreds daily. Dumas appointed Pasteur to a committee to study the outbreak. Pasteur and Claude Bernard examined the ventilation in stricken hospital wards. When a friend and fellow committee member, Henri Sainte-Claire Deville, commented on the courage required to take part in such a study, Pasteur replied in a stern tone that it was a matter of duty. Having experienced so much death in his own family, Pasteur knew the fear and anguish disease could bring. The cholera epidemic passed, though, before they could discover its cause.

In 1866, Pasteur returned to Alès accompanied by some of his best former students: Émile Duclaux, Désiré

Émile Duclaux working at Pasteur's summer lab in Alès. With the aid of a microscope, he studied silkworm eggs for signs of infection. *(Courtesy of Institut Pasteur, Paris.)*

Gernez, and Eugène Maillot. They lodged in a hotel until Maillot found an isolated house at Pont-Gisquet, just outside of town near the slope of Hermitage Mountain. Marie Pasteur joined in Louis's work with her usual dedication. Although she found the worms disgusting— a revulsion shared by her daughters—she learned the skills of silkworm breeders so she could help in the experiments.

Pasteur would always remember Pont-Gisquet fondly. There, he rose at 4:30 each morning, long before the others, to check on the worms in their nurseries, which he insisted be kept scrupulously clean. He prohibited

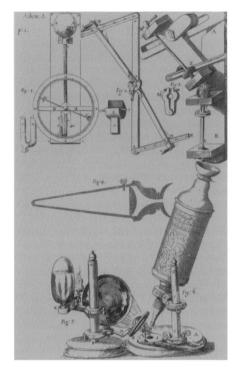

An early model of the microscope. The tool was crucial to Pasteur's understanding of diseases and the microbes that caused them.

sweeping, which raised dust, insisting the floors be washed down with a wet rag instead.

Soon Pasteur began to understand the silkworms' disease. His careful observations and experiments led him to conclude that the corpuscles he thought were symptoms were actually parasites, and the cause of the disease.

Pasteur eventually discovered that pébrine was contagious, spread by contaminated mulberry leaves, the corpuscle-laden dust suspended in the air, the worms scratching each other, or the hands or clothing of caretakers. Pébrine was also passed from a moth to its eggs. Precautions could be taken to prevent the spread of the disease, but because the corpuscles did not appear until an egg had matured, a reliable method of identifying contaminated eggs was needed. Pasteur used his favorite tool, the microscope, to find one.

Pasteur wrote letters to egg merchants and visited silkworm nurseries, explaining his method of egg selection. The silkworm growers needed to separate sick moths from healthy ones. If the microscope revealed that a moth contained the disease-causing corpuscles, all of that moth's eggs would be discarded. Some breeders complained that using a microscope was too hard, to which Pasteur said, "There is in my laboratory a little girl eight years of age who has learned to use it without difficulty." He was talking about his daughter, Marie-Louise. Pasteur's imperial manner did not help his relations with these farmers, who were not always easily convinced to alter their traditional methods.

When not helping Louis in the laboratory, Marie stayed busy taking care of the family. In April 1866, Marie and the girls were in Chambéry visiting Marie's family when twelve-year-old Cécile developed typhoid fever. Alarmed at the news, Pasteur traveled to be with them. After two weeks, Cécile seemed to be recovering, and Louis returned to his lab. Then, in May, a sudden relapse killed Cécile before he could see her again. Like reliving a bad dream, Pasteur made another trip to Arbois to bury a family member. In less than seven years, the Pasteurs had seen three daughters die, and Louis feared his last two children would shortly follow.

When, at the 1867 Universal Exposition in Paris, Pasteur was awarded the grand prize for his studies of wine and the development of pasteurization, observers at the ceremony commented on how somber and sad he looked. He was known around the world for the success of his work, but his health was not good and his family

Marie Pasteur was both companion and collaborator to Louis throughout their long marriage. Shown here in 1867, Marie takes dictation from Louis regarding his research on silkworm diseases. *(Courtesy of Institut Pasteur, Paris.)*

had suffered. As well, Pasteur's relentless self-promotion and desire for fame had him at odds with some of his peers.

Pasteur was still employed at the École Normale as an administrator, even though he neither liked the job nor was well suited to it. He had little sympathy for the students; he thought them frivolous and a waste of his time. The final straw came when one of the students wrote a letter in support of a politician who advocated freedom of thought. The letter was leaked to a newspaper and published. Since the École forbade participation in political activities, Pasteur had the student expelled and intended to also punish those who had circulated the letter. The student body revolted, refusing to provide names and demanding the return of the expelled student. Pasteur's strict policies had been unpopular to begin with and now he was vilified. The students marched into the streets, forcing the school to close. Only the removal of Pasteur and two top administrators finally pacified the students.

Because of Pasteur's reputation as a researcher, he was offered a prestigious position as professor of chemistry at the Sorbonne. Pasteur no longer had to deal with discipline and other administrative duties; he could focus entirely on research.

Still anguished by his children's deaths, Pasteur wrote to the Emperor, asking for money to study contagious diseases. To make more progress, he said, he needed better labs and equipment. Napoleon III agreed, and wrote to the Minister of Education, arranging for a new facility to be built where Pasteur could continue his work. Pasteur was tremendously gratified by the state's recognition of his research, but the money for his new lab was eventually denied and the funds diverted.

In response, Pasteur published a pamphlet blasting the French government for spending millions of francs on a new opera house when scientists worked in dingy, poorly funded, and unhealthy labs. He asserted that a country's strength depended on its scientific accomplishments and that France was falling behind other countries, Germany in particular. Some government officials shared his views and, finally, the money was found. The building of Pasteur's new lab began.

Pasteur returned to Alès and found, to his dismay, that his silkworm research had taken a turn for the worse. The silkworms were still dying. He wrote in his notebook: "In a brood of a hundred worms, I picked up fifteen or twenty dead ones every day, black and rotting with extraordinary rapidity…They were soft and flaccid like an empty bladder. I looked in vain for corpuscles; there was not a trace of them." Silkworm breeders complained bitterly, blaming Pasteur for losses of entire broods.

Typically, Pasteur did not share his research until he was certain of his results. Recent studies of his notebooks confirm that Pasteur withheld the results of hundreds of failed experiments, choosing only to announce his success. While this practice was not unusual, it signifies how important success was to him. Pasteur struggled to understand why his theories were failing. Frustrated after realizing what he had not seen before, he told Duclaux, Gernez, and Maillot: "Nothing is accomplished; there are *two* diseases!"

They were shocked that Pasteur had confided so much to them. Duclaux said of Pasteur after his death: "If he was a discoverer, it was first of all because he was a silent man and an obstinate one." Pasteur's assistants were equally amazed that his confidence was shaken. After recovering, they said: "But, monsieur, what if there are two diseases? That means only that your work is not finished, not that you have accomplished nothing."

Pasteur's drawing of a healthy silkworm larva. *(Courtesy of Institut Pasteur, Paris.)*

Encouraged by their faith in him, Pasteur resumed his experimentation until he finally separated the symptoms of the second disease, *flacherie*, from those of pébrine. Flacherie was characterized by flatulence (gas) and diarrhea, and caused by a different microbe. Now Pasteur and his associates needed to find a different way to identify the disease.

Pasteur noticed that crowded, damp, and poorly ventilated living conditions weakened the worms' ability to fight disease and were ideal for germ growth. While others knew that living conditions were important to health, Pasteur was among the first to understand that cleanliness reduced or eliminated germs. He recommended more space and a constant supply of clean, healthy mulberry leaves. Pasteur also discovered that individual members of a species vary in their receptivity to germs. Finally, he learned that viruses can grow stronger after passing through certain organisms, a fact he would later put to good use.

Then, on the morning of October 19, 1868, Pasteur felt a strange tingling. After lunch he had a shivering fit, which alarmed his family. He insisted on reading a report that afternoon to the Academy of Sciences. Marie, pretending to have shopping to do, accompanied him to the door of the Academy and recruited a friend to walk him home. By nighttime Pasteur could not move his left side. He was only forty-five years old but, like his mother, he had had a stroke.

Pasteur's doctors were puzzled by the strange onset of his paralysis, which came in a series of fits rather than all at once. The famous Dr. Andral prescribed the application of sixteen leeches behind the ears. After the letting of much blood, his doctor wrote: "Speech clearer, some movements of the paralyzed limbs; intelligence perfect." That evening Pasteur complained about his arm being heavy as lead and completely useless, so useless he wished it could be cut off. The medical note described him as extremely cold, anxious, and agitated. His features appeared depressed, and his eyes unfocused and languid. He slept so deeply that, in the middle of the night, Marie feared he was dying.

Pasteur woke at dawn on October 21, no longer drowsy. His doctor wrote at mid-day: "Mental faculties still absolutely intact." And two hours later: "Mind active; would willingly talk science." Pasteur later dictated to Gernez, who had tried in vain to distract him, a note on a method for discovering eggs vulnerable to flacherie. The paper was read at the Academy of Sciences exactly one week after Pasteur's stroke.

Many feared that Pasteur would not recover. When he asked from his bed how the building of the lab was progressing, his wife and Marie-Louise answered only vaguely. Pasteur soon realized that the construction had been abandoned. When a friend, a high-ranking government official, stopped by for a visit, Pasteur said

Bloodletting continued to be a popular treatment for a variety of ailments even in Pasteur's time. *(From a fifteenth century Italian medical textbook.)*

bitterly that it would have been more straightforward to say that the work had been suspended because they thought he would die. The Emperor was informed of Pasteur's distress and ordered the building to be resumed immediately.

Concerned for his health, Louis's wife and daughter tried in vain to keep him from working. Friends came by to read to him from books on philosophy and religion. Two months after the stroke he made it, with help, to the dining room for dinner. A week later, he took his first, shaky, unassisted steps. Just three months after the stroke, against the advice of doctors, family, friends, and colleagues, he insisted on returning to work.

Pasteur traveled back to Alès from Paris in a modified train compartment. He continued his silkworm studies with his left side still mostly paralyzed. His forearm was bent and contracted, his fingers clenched and immobilized, and his leg stiff. This partial paralysis would stay with him the rest of his life, making it necessary to have more assistance in the lab. Pasteur's nephew, Adrien Loir, who later served as his laboratory assistant and, in Marie's absence, his personal valet, wrote: "I became his tool, the indispensable accessory that he would use as he saw fit without encountering resistance or opposition."

Because he did not always study the classic or fashionable scientific questions, working for Pasteur was considered a risky career move, and he had difficulty keeping assistants. He created his own science; his students either followed his lead or left. Pasteur was a demanding master who saw his students largely as tools to further his own means. Duclaux later wrote: "Could Pasteur really have collaborators? The term collaborator implies working together, continual exchanges, constant intellectual communication in pursuit of a shared goal, and mutual help. Pasteur never told his entourage anything about what he was doing." Loir offered similar testimony.

As Pasteur's symptoms gradually improved, his family life and lab life blended. In the morning, from his bed, he directed his assistants on their work for the day, and in the afternoon, dictated to Marie for a book entitled *Studies on the Diseases of Silkworms*. No matter his physical condition, Pasteur's work would go on.

Pasteur's work with silkworms was still not a total success. Many breeders had benefited from his advice, but it was not foolproof. When it failed they continued to blame him for their losses.

The controversy only seemed to encourage Pasteur. His confidence ran high. The government sent him eggs to test, which he quickly concluded were bad without bothering to test them. His critics wondered why Pasteur had disposed of the eggs rather than allow them to develop and support his claim. The Lyons Silk Commission had its doubts, as well. In March of 1869 they asked Pasteur for a sample of eggs he would guarantee to be healthy. He went beyond their request and provided four samples, with four specific predictions: healthy, pébrineladen, flacherie-laden, and both pébrine- and flacherie-laden. Each of the samples developed precisely as he predicted.

Impressed by the news that Pasteur appeared to have conquered the silkworm diseases, Napoleon III arranged for Louis and his family to go to Villa Vicentina, in Italy, which was plagued by silkworm illnesses. Napoleon III's son owned the villa, and Pasteur's success or failure there would alter the course of his career. After eight months under Pasteur's guidance, the silkworms produced a profit for the first time in a decade.

During his stay at Villa Vicentina, Pasteur continued writing his book on silkworm diseases. He sometimes agonized over whether he would ever fully recover from his stroke. He wrote to a friend: "I am alive, that is all I can say. Can I hope to return to normal? Yes and no. When my head is clear, I forget the past and make plans for the future. I see myself surrounded by collaborators in a beautiful, spacious laboratory... I even indulge in the idea that some day I will recover the use of my hand. But sometimes my head is muddled and heavy, and then I despair, and all I want is to go off to die in some hidden corner."

While Pasteur struggled to find satisfaction in his work, events were unfolding on a global scale that would threaten his happiness further. In July of 1870, the war between France and Prussia erupted and, before its conclusion, France's strength would be severely tested.

CHAPTER SIX
ANTHRAX

In 1870, Prussia was the largest of the states that would eventually combine to form Germany. Relations between France and Prussia had been uneasy for some time, but the turning point came when a Prussian prince was offered the throne of Spain. French protest of the offer prevented it from happening, but only increased the mounting tension between the two powers. For the fourth time in one hundred years, Prussia and France entered into battle. Prussia's large, well-trained army quickly defeated French forces on many fronts. The Prussian army rolled across the French countryside and marched on Paris, capturing Napoleon III along the way.

Pasteur returned to Paris. He wanted to join the National Guard and had to be reminded that being half-paralyzed made him unfit for duty. Bertin, who was caring for the wounded at the École Normale, urged Pasteur to leave the city, as he would be only another mouth to feed during the coming siege. His heart aching, Pasteur traveled to Arbois.

He wrote to the editor of a Paris paper:

> I have only one way to express my support for our valiant soldiers who are arising en masse to drive out the foreigner. I am sending you another gift of 100

Edouard Detaille's *Combat à Villejeuif (Siège de Paris), 19 Septembre 1870,* depicts the French soldiers' vain attempts to hold off the Prussian invasion of the barricaded city. The soldiers seem to be watching almost passively as the unseeable force approaches. *(Courtesy of Musée d'Orsay, Paris.)*

Pasteur's next challenge was to understand how anthrax spread. Koch's experiments had shown that anthrax spores could survive for many years, but when the
old spores were fed to animals, some developed anthrax
and some did not. Pasteur repeated these experiments
and found that the animals developing anthrax had also
eaten prickly plants. He then theorized the anthrax
spores had invaded the animal's blood through tiny cuts
in their mouths caused by the dry, sharp food.

Knowing how the anthrax spores got into the animals'
blood did not help to explain where the anthrax spores
originated. Shepherds, who knew the grazing patterns
of their animals intimately, considered some fields to be
cursed. Pasteur listened to the shepherds and realized
that anthrax-infested animals had been buried in those
fields, but that did not explain how simply grazing there
could make healthy animals sick—after all, the corpses
were buried deep underground.

Near Chartres, Pasteur watched animals in the fields
for hours, certain the answer was out there. One day
Pasteur was in the fields when he noticed the tiny,
familiar cylinders of soil signaling the tunneling of
earthworms. Looking at the freshly turned dirt, Pasteur
realized it might be possible that the worms carried the
anthrax spores from the dead bodies underground to the
surface of the earth, thus contaminating the fields.

Pasteur collected earthworms from the "cursed" fields.
He studied the contents of their intestines and found
they contained anthrax spores. Earthworms process

organic materials through their digestive tracts and their waste fertilizes soil, eventually making its way into animals through that soil. Pasteur recommended that anthrax-infected corpses be burned, or else buried in ground inhospitable to earthworms, such as limestone or sand.

Pasteur still had to lobby for the public acceptance of his findings. Gabriel Colin, a professor of veterinarian medicine, was a constant critic. He and Pasteur would exchange many dramatic challenges and insults over the years, particularly when Pasteur presented his anthrax findings to the Academy of Medicine (to which Pasteur, the chemist, had been elected in 1873).

In spite of these and many other challenges to his findings, Pasteur's reputation was on the rise, and one of the most significant discoveries of his career was still to come. In his studies, Pasteur had noticed that the animals that recovered from mild anthrax became immune to the disease. He would go on to combine these findings with the work of English doctor Edward Jenner to develop a method for saving many lives.

CHAPTER SEVEN
VACCINES

Pasteur had always been fascinated by disease, and his children's deaths only intensified his desire to conquer it. He wrote, "How I wish I had enough health and sufficient knowledge to throw myself body and soul into the experimental study of one of our infectious diseases." His work with fermentation gave him his first clue about disease: aseptic, or sterile, methods kept undesired microbes out of wine, for instance, and prevented spoilage from occurring. Similarly, if sheep did not ingest anthrax spores, they did not develop anthrax. Pasteur reasoned that microbes could be responsible for illness in humans as well.

Pasteur became vigilant about cleanliness and avoiding germs. When passing near a hospital with family, he made them cover their mouths with handkerchiefs. He would swerve into the street, dragging his companion with him, to avoid dust shaken out of mops from first-floor windows. He examined dishes for dust, and typically rinsed plates before using them. Pasteur apparently had a phobia of shaking hands, and in cases where the gesture could not be avoided, he would immediately wash his hands with soap. Rather than use hand-towels, virtual havens for germs, he used special disposable papers.

Pasteur was not the first to notice a link between sanitation and disease. Two doctors, Oliver Wendell Holmes in the United States and Ignaz Semmelweiss in Austria, believed disease could be spread by doctors' dirty hands. Both faced harsh ridicule for their theories. People continued to die of infection as minor operations often led to gangrene, amputation, and death. Soldiers died from infected wounds, and women, after giving birth in hospitals, frequently developed fevers and died.

Childbirth fever had intrigued Pasteur since the wife of Émile Duclaux, his collaborator and former student, died from it. With typical thoroughness, Pasteur went looking for the cause. He began in the hospitals, using his trusty microscope, and he was not surprised by his findings. He found circular germs that grew in chains and were spread from one patient to another by doctors' hands, instruments, sponges, and dressings. Many doctors refused to believe Pasteur, who said grimly, "I shall force them to see; they will have to see."

Pasteur embarked on a campaign to clean up hospitals. He instructed doctors on sterilization techniques. He showed them to use heat to clean their instruments by passing them through a flame and recommended frequent hand washing. Not every doctor was convinced, and even those who were sometimes had trouble implementing these new methods. Pasteur once saw a well-intentioned doctor flame his scalpel, let it cool, then wipe it on his dirty, germ-covered apron, as he was accustomed to doing.

Joseph Lister's ideas about antiseptics changed the way medicine was practiced in the late 1800s. *(Courtesy of Medicinhistoriska Museét, Stockholm, Sweden.)*

Doctors naturally resisted the idea that they had inadvertently caused so much death. Many insisted that disease was a spontaneous chemical process originating from within, rather than the result of microbial invasions. Because clinical medicine was not closely associated with laboratory science, many doctors were angered that Pasteur, a mere chemist, criticized their procedures. One doctor even contaminated wounds on purpose—and then bragged about it—in an attempt to

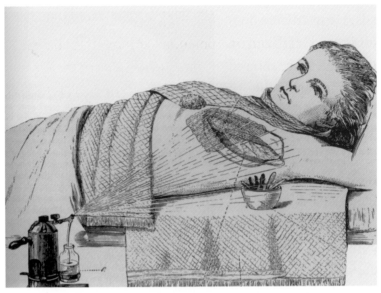

The Lister method for antiseptic surgery involved spraying carbolic gas on the open wound to protect against infection. *(Courtesy of Wellcome Institute Library, London.)*

prove the ineffectiveness of good hygiene.

There were some medical professionals who took Pasteur's side. One surgeon wrote, "A pin-prick is a door open to Death." If a pinprick was a door, then surgery was rolling out the welcome mat. An English surgeon, Joseph Lister, developed an antiseptic method for surgery, using carbolic acid in the operating room to kill bacteria that might infect wounds. He wrote to Pasteur, thanking him for his research in germ theory and fermentation, crediting this work as inspiring his own discoveries. Lister's method drastically increased surgery survival rates.

The work that Pasteur began pointed the way toward future scientific developments. He observed that certain bacteria inhibited the growth of others—almost fifty years before Alexander Fleming discovered penicillin and realized its potential for treating bacterial infections. He also saw the possibility of epidemics spreading from continent to continent, and had to struggle against mistaken ideas regarding the origins of disease. Many scientists and doctors remained tied to the idea that disease arose spontaneously. Pasteur would not let the issue drop, even though his colleagues begged him. He was determined to win the fight against the "medical doctrine which I believe to be fatal to progress in the art of healing—the doctrine of the spontaneity of all diseases...."

In 1878, Pasteur was at the Academy of Medicine when an older doctor began to speak about spontaneous causes of childbirth fever. Pasteur could not contain himself, and called out "None of those things cause the epidemic...It is the nursing and medical staff who carry the microbe from an infected woman to a healthy one." The older doctor was put off by Pasteur's rudeness, and replied that he doubted he would live long enough to see such a microbe discovered. Pasteur rose, limped up

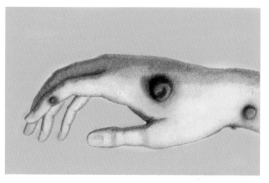

Cowpox caused painful sores to develop all over the body. Once a person contracted the disease, they seemed to be immune to the even more painful, fatal smallpox. This realization would lead to the first vaccine. *(Courtesy of the Wellcome Institute Library, London.)*

Edward Jenner pioneered the development of vaccines. His work was crucial to Pasteur's progress with rabies. *(Courtesy of Wellcome Institute Library, London.)*

to the blackboard, and emphatically drew the round germs in chains (now known as streptococcus) he had found in his study of childbirth fever.

The next day, the old doctor invited Pasteur to his hospital clinic, and soon Pasteur became a frequent visitor. Pasteur's assistant, Émile Roux, later wrote of these visits:

> No one knows what feelings of repulsion Pasteur had to overcome before visiting patients and witnessing postmortem examinations. His sensibility was extreme, and he suffered morally and physically from the pains of others; the cut of the bistoury (a small surgical knife) opening an abscess made him wince as if he himself had received it…we have often seen him go home ill from these operating theatres. But his love of science, his desire for truth were the stronger; he returned the next day.

A doctor and his assistant vaccinate rural women and children against smallpox, using the vaccine developed by Edward Jenner. *(Reinhard Zimmerman, 1857. Courtesy of Bildarchiv Preussischer Kulturbesitz, Berlin.)*

There, Pasteur developed the first bacterial cultures using blood samples, a diagnostic technique used in present-day medicine. He also convinced one old doctor to change his opinion about hygiene.

Good hygiene meant eliminating exposure to microbes. A second method of disease prevention involved the opposite technique: the deliberate introduction of microbes. People had long recognized that some contagious diseases could be caught only once, but the reason for this remained a mystery. In the late 1700s, the English surgeon Edward Jenner observed that milkmaids who developed cowpox, a mild disease, later seemed to be resistant to the similar, but more lethal, smallpox. To test whether cowpox made people immune, he injected cowpox into an eight-year-old boy, then inoculated him with smallpox. The boy remained healthy. Jenner's amazing vaccine, from the Latin *vacca*, meaning cow, prevented countless people from dying of smallpox.

Most diseases, though, do not have a milder twin. Nearly a century had passed since Jenner's great discovery. Thousands of people, including two of Pasteur's daughters, had died from diseases such as cholera, polio, yellow fever, and typhoid. The goal of prevention was never far from Pasteur's mind and, while studying chickens affected by cholera, he arrived at a new idea.

Chicken cholera could wipe out ninety percent of a flock in days. Jean-Joseph-Henri Toussaint, a veterinarian studying the disease, found microbes in the blood of infected chickens and asked for Pasteur's help. Once Pasteur confirmed that the microbe identified by Toussaint caused the disease, he discovered that guinea pigs served as carriers, spreading the microbes without perishing from the disease, much as earthworms did with anthrax. The next step was to try to find a way to prevent it.

Pasteur spent the summer of 1879 in Arbois, as was his custom. His assistants Charles Chamberland and Émile Roux continued to work on chicken cholera in his absence, taking the opportunity to try some ideas of their own. When Pasteur returned in the fall, Roux had something to show him. He had discovered that a culture of the microbes that caused chicken cholera could be weakened if it was exposed to the air for some period of time. When he injected this weakened culture into chickens, they did not get sick. And when he then injected those same chickens with a lethal dose from a fresh culture, they still did not get sick. Remarkably, the discovery implied that deliberately introducing weakened bacteria into a healthy chicken protected the bird from stronger forms of the same disease. It was not necessary, then, for a disease to have a weaker twin (such as cowpox to smallpox) in order to make a vaccine.

Émile Roux contributed greatly to Pasteur's research. As an assistant to the famous scientist, Roux often failed to receive proper recognition for his original work and ideas. *(Courtesy of Musée Pasteur, Paris.)*

Pasteur's laboratory notes clearly show that Roux

was responsible for this discovery, but Roux was an assistant and Pasteur, the famous scientist, took full credit. He told the public both accident and intellect contributed to his find: it was an accident that the culture was weakened and his intellect that suggested giving those same chickens another dose. Roux's feelings about losing the credit for his discovery are not known, but he remained loyal to Pasteur and it is likely that he accepted the usurping as his master's right. This is not the only known instance of Pasteur borrowing from Roux, and it seems fair to guess that his other assistants had their work appropriated as well.

Pasteur and his assistants continued to work at refining their method of preventing chicken cholera. They called the protective inoculations "vaccines" in honor of Edward Jenner's cowpox vaccine. Once chicken cholera had been conquered, they returned their attention to anthrax.

Anthrax was different from chicken cholera because it also attacked humans. Eliminating anthrax in animals would bring science closer to protecting humans from the deadly spores. Pasteur was optimistic:

> If it is terrifying to think that life may be at the mercy of the multiplication of those infinitesimally small creatures, it is also consoling to hope that Science will not always remain powerless before such enemies, since having barely begun the study of them, she has taught us, for example, that simple contact with the air is sometimes sufficient to destroy them…"

Inoculating sheep against anthrax, as illustrated in an 1882 Paris magazine.

But exposing anthrax to air did nothing: the bacteria simply formed into tough spores.

Pasteur varied the conditions in experiment after experiment, searching for a way around the incredibly resistant spores. In July 1880, his last sister, Virginie, died of a stroke. He was acutely aware of the shadow of death over his family but worked on. Finally, his perseverance paid off. He discovered that, at a certain temperature, anthrax bacteria would grow without forming spores. They could be weakened at that temperature. Sheep injected with the diminished germs became only mildly sick, and then recovered. Once they did, they were immune to the full-strength anthrax germs. Pasteur had created a second vaccine.

The next important discovery came soon after, when Pasteur found that weakened anthrax bacteria, when

dried, created weakened spores. Normal spores protected and spread deadly anthrax, but these weakened
spores could be the key to preventing the disease. They
could also be easily produced and shipped around the
world.

Pasteur announced his findings to the Academy of
Sciences. In his inimitable fashion, he did so without
divulging his procedures. Naturally, his critics scoffed.
Jean-Pierre Rossignol, the editor of the *Veterinary Press*,
had recently published an article mocking Pasteur's
close-mouthed, arrogant style: "Microbiolatry is the
fashion, it reigns undisputed; it is a doctrine which must
not even be discussed, especially when its Pontiff, the
learned M. Pasteur, has pronounced the sacred words, 'I
have spoken...' the microbe alone is true, and Pasteur
is its prophet."

When Rossignol heard Pasteur's claim to have an
anthrax vaccine, he began to collect money to sponsor
a large-scale test. He offered his own farm, Pouilly le
Fort, near Melun. Pasteur's assistants cautioned him
against such a public test, fearing their work was not yet
ready for scrutiny, but Pasteur insisted they go on.

On May 5, 1881, in the presence of a large crowd of
farmers, veterinarians, doctors, and reporters, Pasteur
directed his assistants to give the vaccine to twenty-four
sheep, six cows, and one goat, and to withhold the
vaccine from the same number of animals. Two weeks
later, a second, stronger vaccine was given, and in the
final test, on May 31, both vaccinated and unvaccinated

animals were injected with powerful anthrax bacteria. Pasteur boldly predicted that all vaccinated animals would survive, and that all unvaccinated animals would die.

Gabriel Colin, Pasteur's old foe, remained as distrustful as ever. Colin had told a veterinarian named Biot, who would be present for the final injections, that after the strong germs settled to the bottom of the fluid, Pasteur would give the weakest part on the top to the vaccinated animals and the strongest part on the bottom to the unvaccinated, thus biasing the test in his favor. Colin advised shaking the vials prior to the injections. Biot not only shook the vials, he asked that a double dose be administered. Pasteur, betraying no emotion, ordered a triple dose.

Pasteur returned home for the torturous wait. The next day, his veneer of calm vanished when he heard that a few vaccinated sheep seemed ill. He berated Roux, afraid that carelessness had ruined the results and his own reputation. Haggard, he paced the floor, muttering to himself. Marie's attempts to reassure him were futile. He feared failure: animals dying, public humiliation, months wasted on a useless vaccine.

On the morning of June 2, Rossignol's telegram arrived declaring the test a "stunning success." With his family and assistants, Pasteur traveled to Pouilly le Fort, where the vaccinated sheep had indeed recovered and the unvaccinated animals lay dead and dying. Farmers, shepherds, scientists, townspeople, politicians, and news

applied for a patent and then put it into the public domain for everyone's benefit. When Napoleon III had asked Pasteur why he did not sell his patents, he said he did not pursue science for personal gain, that business concerns would only distract him from scientific questions.

The French government had decided, in 1874, to give Pasteur a recompense of 12,000 francs annually, and in 1883 that amount was increased to 25,000 francs. Colleagues urged him to retire, to focus on his health and his family, but for Pasteur, the money meant freedom to pursue his research. From his earliest days he had trained himself to focus on his work. Now, an old man, it did not seem possible he could do anything else. He wrote: "Let me tell you the secret that has led me to the goal. My only strength resides in my tenacity." On their wedding anniversary that year, Marie wrote to their children: "Your father is absorbed in his thoughts, talks little, sleeps little, rises at dawn, and, in one word, continues the life I began with him this day thirty-five years ago."

Pasteur's fame continued to grow. Schools and streets were dedicated to his name and he received hundreds of letters from people across the world thanking him for his work. He also received hundreds more from people begging him to find cures for other diseases. Pasteur read those letters and felt anew the pain of losing three children. He wanted to help. Rabies, the plague of his childhood, gave him a chance.

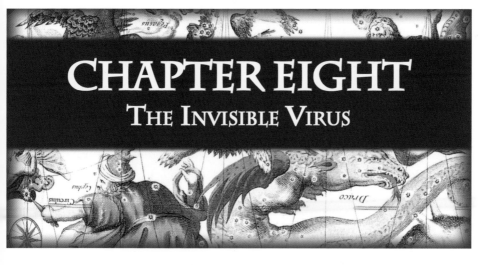

CHAPTER EIGHT
THE INVISIBLE VIRUS

As it had in Pasteur's youth, rabies still filled villages with panic and terror. The disease usually arrived in an area when a rabid animal, often a dog or a wolf, staggered in and proceeded to ravage the town. While the number of people contracting rabies through bites from infected animals was not high, the disease was virtually always fatal. Victims suffered from breathlessness, a tormenting thirst confounded by an inability to swallow, and horrible spasms. Only death brought relief. Because victims could not drink, rabies was sometimes called hydrophobia, meaning fear of water.

The only treatment that had any success was to immediately burn all the flesh in and surrounding the bite wound. Called cauterization, it was the treatment Pasteur had witnessed as a boy when the blacksmith used

Cauterizing irons and a wound receiving the painful treatment, in a sixteenth-century German woodcut. *(Courtesy of the Philadelphia Museum of Art, Philadelphia.)*

a red-hot iron. Other attempts at cures were even less effective: sea water, eyes of crayfish, droppings of red roosters, swallows' nests, the burnt hair of a bear, shrews' tails, and all sorts of herbs.

The cause of the disease, like so many others, was unknown. There seemed to be a connection between the animal's symptoms, its bite, and the resulting symptoms in the bitten person. Out of fear that the disease was transmittable from person to person, victims of rabies had often been killed in order to stop its spread. Pasteur turned his attention to his microscope, as he had so many

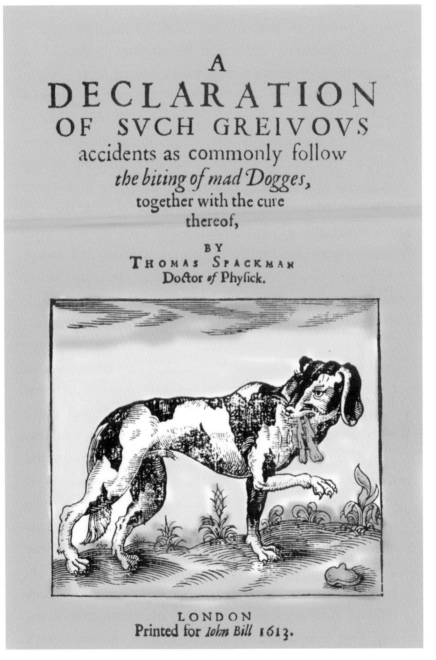

A
DECLARATION
OF SVCH GREIVOVS
accidents as commonly follow
the biting of mad Dogges,
together with the cure
thereof,

BY
THOMAS SPACKMAN
Doctor *of* Phyfick.

LONDON
Printed for *Iohn Bill* 1613.

This title page from a 1613 treatise on rabies vividly illustrates the fear the disease
generated. *(Courtesy of the Royal Society of Medicine, London.)*

times before, to look for the cause of the disease.

The symptoms implicated the nervous system. If a rabies microbe existed, it probably lurked there. Scientists would later discover rabies is caused by a virus, a particle too small for the equipment of Pasteur's era to detect. In experiment after experiment, Pasteur saw nothing out of the ordinary through the lens of his microscope. He and his assistants began to look for a new way to isolate rabies. It was Roux who made the first breakthrough. He placed brain tissue from rabid animals directly onto the brains of healthy animals and rabies developed every time, confirming that the cause could be found in the nervous system of infected animals. Still, they had not found a way to prevent the disease.

Pasteur's efforts at conquering rabies were not producing results as he had hoped. He knew of no way to produce a vaccine if he could not isolate the particle that caused it. The aging scientist grew more and more melancholy as each of his attempts failed. The project would be resuscitated, not by Pasteur but, once again, by Roux.

Pasteur's nephew, Adrien Loir, recalled Pasteur once coming upon a flask in which Roux had suspended part of a rabbit's spinal cord. Realizing Roux had found a way to weaken the virus by exposing it to air, Pasteur quickly appropriated the technique as his own. Roux later saw three of Pasteur's flasks containing much the same work, and Loir confirmed that Pasteur had viewed Roux's experiment. Furious, Roux stormed out of the lab.

Roux had grown tired of Pasteur usurping his ideas. He stopped working on the rabies project and no longer came to the lab when Pasteur was there, but he could not bring himself to break with Pasteur entirely. Roux continued to champion Pasteur's work and would later assume leadership of the Pasteur Institute after Louis's death.

Creating a weakened strain of rabies virus by exposing the spinal cord of an infected rabbit to the air led to the vaccine's development. *(Courtesy of Institut Pasteur.)*

Pasteur was unmoved by Roux's anger. He appropriated Roux's technique and soon had a reliable vaccine. The dried spinal cords could be ground up to create a series of injections that began as very weak forms of the rabies microbe and gradually grew stronger over a period of two weeks. After undergoing the fourteen injections, dogs injected with fresh rabies virus did not get sick—an astounding scientific achievement.

Pasteur presented his paper on rabies at the International Medical Congress in Copenhagen, where his son, Jean-Baptiste, was secretary to the French Legation. When he finished, the distinguished audience erupted into applause. Everyone wondered whether the vaccine was ready for humans, but Pasteur still felt more research was needed.

Pasteur wanted more than a preventive vaccine. Since the number of actual rabies cases was low, it was not practical to vaccinate everyone who might be exposed to it; it would be better to have a way to treat bite victims. Rabies had a long incubation period (the time it took for the virus to travel from the bite wound to the brain). This gave Pasteur the idea to create a vaccine that could stimulate immunity quickly, before the virus could reach the brain.

Working with silkworms, Pasteur had found that the strength of a bacterial or viral strain increased or decreased in successive passages through different animal species. By passing the rabies virus through rabbits, Pasteur developed a potent rabies strain, strong enough to stimulate the immune system faster than the natural virus, then weakened it so it could not cause the disease. The vaccination consisted of fourteen daily shots, beginning with the oldest and weakest strain (fourteen days old) and gradually building to the freshest and strongest (zero days old, not weakened at all).

In order to produce and test a rabies vaccine, Pasteur and his laboratory needed a constant supply of the virus. They kept a number of animals on hand to serve as incubators. Dogs, rabbits, guinea pigs, monkeys, and other animals infected with rabies by the scientists died in the name of rabies research. The antivivisection movement, which was against animal experimentation, was gaining popularity in England, France and the United States. Pasteur and other scientists heard harsh criticism for their experiments on animals, but vigorously defended their practices as necessary. The debate over experimenting on animals continues today. While scientists argue that the deaths of a few animals can lead to improved lives for many people, their opponents say it is unethical to harm innocents and that the biology of animals is too different from humans to provide conclusive evidence.

As his work on rabies became well known, people began to offer themselves to Pasteur as subjects for inoculation. Despite his success with a vaccine in animals, Pasteur was not certain it would work on people, and he turned them down. He wrote to Jules Vercel: "I have not yet dared to treat humans bitten by rabid dogs. But the time to do it may not be far off, and I would really like to begin with myself...."

As news of the potential vaccine spread, solicitations poured in from all over the world. The Emperor of Brazil wrote to ask whether the vaccine was ready for humans. Pasteur responded: "Even when I have multiplied examples of prophylaxis [prevention] of rabies in dogs, I believe that my hand will tremble when it comes to deal with man." He knew that different species can respond differently to chemicals, and if the rabies vaccine was too strong, the person receiving it would die.

Pasteur was caught in a dilemma. Those who had been bitten by a rabid animal did not always develop rabies, but if they did, they died. Pasteur now had a method that he believed could save someone after being bitten, but it had to be administered quickly, before rabies had a chance to take hold. Since rabies could not be detected until symptoms appeared, the person receiving the vaccine would not know whether or not she was infected before opting to receive the potentially fatal shots. But if the person went untreated and developed rabies, she would die.

Julie-Antoinette Poughon was eleven years old when a rabid dog bit her. A month later, she was already beginning to exhibit the symptoms of rabies when her parents sought help from Pasteur. Certain she was already infected and therefore going to die, Pasteur consented to try to treat the girl. Julie-Antoinette did not live through the experiment, but there is no way to know if it was the disease or the vaccination shots that killed her. Julie-Antoinette's treatment was kept a secret for fear her death would bring Pasteur's critics out in droves.

It was less than a month later, in July 1885, that nine-year-old Joseph Meister first arrived in Paris with his mother. A rabid dog had bitten Joseph only two days earlier, and they begged for Pasteur's help. Pasteur agonized over the decision, but in the end decided the possibility of saving the boy's life made the risk worth taking. Joseph received his series of injections and survived.

Pasteur was relieved and triumphant. In later treatments, he would not give patients the last, most potent, injection, but in Joseph's case it proved the vaccine had been a success.

The news of Joseph Meister's recovery spread and the lab was flooded with pleas for help, but Pasteur refused them, still not convinced his vaccine was ready for the public. The story of another young boy motivated him to act.

A wild dog had attacked Jean-Baptiste Jupille, a fifteen-year-old shepherd boy from a small town near Arbois. Armed with only a whip, he held the deranged dog off, its foaming mouth clamped onto his left hand, until several younger shepherd boys could get away. The boy then threw the dog to the ground and wrested his hand free. He bound the dog's jaws with his whip, clubbed it with his wooden shoe, and drowned it in a nearby stream. Jupille suffered several deep bites during the struggle, and the dog's autopsy confirmed it had rabies. By the time Jupille arrived in Paris, six days had elapsed since the incident.

The sight of the wounds shocked Pas-

Jean-Baptiste Jupille in 1885. *(Burndy Library, Dibner Center, Cambridge, Mass.)*

teur. His sympathy went out to the boy, but he questioned whether the vaccine would be too late, or worse, would hasten the development of rabies. Sure that the boy had been exposed to the virus, Pasteur felt compelled to take the risk. He knew Meister's treatment was successful and thought Jupille should be treated as well.

Three months after Meister's vaccination, and only a week into Jupille's treatment, Pasteur reported to the Academy of Sciences that he had developed a cure for rabies. It is surprising that Pasteur did not wait for Jupille's injections to be finished before announcing his findings, but, as usual, he had faith in his work. Jupille survived, but not all of Pasteur's peers were convinced of the vaccine's safety or effectiveness. Some raved about his miraculous success; others, including Roux, felt he had prematurely treated humans. Once again, Pasteur's results were eclipsed by debates about his methodology and the high-handed way he presented his findings.

In the years since Pasteur first proclaimed a cure, his laboratory notebooks have been unearthed and examined. Their analysis has led to two major criticisms of his work. First, his research results had not been entirely consistent on the question of whether to move from the weakest to the strongest virus, or vice versa. He had obtained positive results going from weak to strong, but did not have time to repeat the experiment before Joseph Meister knocked on his laboratory door. In his defense, no ethical guidelines existed about when to try new treatments. Individual clinical judgment reigned su-

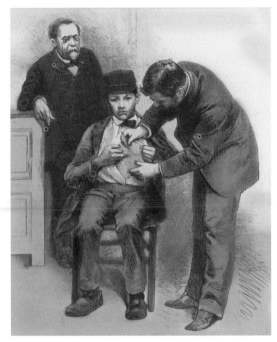

After being attacked by a rabid dog, Jean-Baptiste Jupille received the rabies vaccination while Pasteur looked on. *(Courtesy of Institut Pasteur, Paris.)*

preme, and many other medical procedures then in use had spent even less time in the lab before being tried on humans.

The second criticism involved the death of Julie-Antoinette Poughon. Her death was never made public, which was often the case with negative results, and critics argue Pasteur acted recklessly when he vaccinated Joseph Meister so soon after the girl's death. If Joseph Meister's family knew that another child had died, they might not have been so eager for their son to have the same treatment. In his own time, Pasteur was called a hero; in retrospect, we might see his actions in a slightly different light. Now we have governmental organizations to oversee the safety and results of experiments, and drugs and vaccines must undergo rigorous testing before being approved for human use. Joseph Meister and Jean-Baptiste Jupille would have died if Pasteur had been required to follow our modern protocols.

Pasteur created a rabies treatment center where he and his assistants worked long hours to make as much vaccine as possible. News of Pasteur's success traveled quickly, and bite victims from Algeria, England, Germany, Hungary, Italy, Russia and Spain flocked to France to be saved. Patients came from across the ocean: four children from Newark, New Jersey were bitten by a marauding dog and shipped to Pasteur, their passage paid by donations from concerned citizens. They were treated, and all survived. Pasteur's fame spread as newspapers across America made him front-page news for weeks after the boys returned home, safe and alive.

Pasteur and his assistants took great care with their vaccines but, even so, a small number of treatments failed. Some patients were likely allergic to the rabies virus, and others began treatment too late. One such patient's father later wrote of Pasteur, "Among the great men about whose life I have been able to learn, none seems greater to me. I do not see one of them capable, as he was in the case of our dear little girl, of sacrificing long years of work, of endangering a universal reputation as a scientist and knowingly risking a painful failure, out of simple humanity."

Not everyone was as convinced. Articles in the press

News of Pasteur's successful rabies vaccination spread quickly.
Though his work was often criticized, it was nearly as often praised.
Here he is depicted as a great hero, saving children from rabid dogs.
(Courtesy of Institut Pasteur, Paris.)

frequently attacked Pasteur and his work. In the Academy of Medicine, the rabies treatment was described as involuntary manslaughter. Criticism was nothing new to Pasteur, though, and his laboratory worked on.

Pasteur's continued poor health sent him to Italy for the winter of 1886-87. He kept up with the laboratory by mail. One day, a letter brought the news that a man was accusing Pasteur of killing his son. The boy's autopsy, attended by both Grancher and Loir, found he died of kidney disease. But his father took his story to the press, and Émile Roux, who had kept away from the lab since Pasteur plagiarized his methods, realized that the laboratory was threatened and Pasteur was in no shape to defend it. Roux publicly supported the autopsy findings and the matter was eventually dropped. Pasteur is notorious, today, for his inability to admit mistakes or failures, which lends some credence to the possibility the autopsy report was false, but whether the cause of the boy's death was covered up is impossible to know.

Pasteur's stay in Italy was cut short by an earthquake. The first shock hit at 6:30 a.m. on February 23, and Pasteur and his family soon boarded a train for Arbois. Back in his childhood home, in the familiar countryside, Pasteur was able to relax. There, people called him by his first name. They came to him with barrels of spoiled wine, and he took great pleasure in helping them. Roux once said, "Pasteur's work is admirable and proves his genius, but one had to live in his house to fully recognize the goodness of his heart." Pasteur also had many requests for help from people believing him to be a medical doctor. A French novelist, Edmund About, explained to a visitor: "He does not cure individuals. He only tries to cure humanity."

Pasteur's lab continued to vaccinate people bitten by rabid and potentially rabid animals. His vaccine received a thorough examination and vetting from the French rabies commission. A highly respected English commission, which included Sir James Paget and Joseph Lister, scrutinized Pasteur's methods for fourteen months and finally agreed that Pasteur's findings were indeed valid. After so many insults and criticisms, this report gave him deep satisfaction.

Pasteur had returned to Paris, where his small lab was overwhelmed with the volume of patients. He went before the Academy of Sciences to present the accumulated results of his treatments. He proposed the founding of an anti-rabies vaccination center where scientists from France and around the world could be trained and perform research. He refused to accept any money from the city of Paris or the French republic for the center, wanting to be independent of the government.

A subscription for donations was opened, and money

The original building of the Pasteur Institute. *(Courtesy of Institut Pasteur, Paris.)*

poured in from all parts of the world. Donations ranged from a soldier's single franc to one hundred thousand francs from the czar of Russia. The emperor of Brazil and the sultan of Turkey also sent hefty sums, and Pasteur himself contributed one hundred thousand francs. Alsace-Lorraine, home to Joseph Meister and the region that Germany had taken from France in the Franco-Prussian War, donated 48,365 francs in Meister's name.

The Pasteur Institute opened in 1888. It was an enormous building, on a fine site selected by his old student Duclaux. At the inauguration ceremony Pasteur welcomed students, colleagues, and dignitaries from France and abroad.

Pasteur's mind was still sharp but his speech had been weakened by recent strokes. When the time came for his address, Pasteur's son, Jean-Baptiste, read his father's expression of gratitude and his plea for scientific rigor:

> Always cultivate the spirit of criticism…What I am here asking of you…is the most difficult thing the inventor has to learn. To believe that one has found an important scientific fact and to be consumed by the desire to announce it, and yet to be constrained to combat this impulse for days, weeks, sometimes years, to endeavor to ruin one's own experiments, and to announce one's discovery only after one has laid to rest all the contrary hypotheses, yes, that is indeed an arduous task. But when after all these efforts one finally achieves certainty, one feels one of the deepest joys it is given to the human soul to experience.

CHAPTER NINE
PASTEUR PASSES ON

Louis and Marie Pasteur moved into an apartment in a private wing at the Pasteur Institute. All day long, scientists worked in beautiful, new laboratories under Pasteur's watchful eye. His health was in decline but he gamely limped through the corridors, keeping in touch with all the work being done. The center continued to produce rabies vaccinations, train doctors, and perform research on other infectious diseases. Today, the Pasteur Institute continues its founder's mission to make life better for the citizens of the world.

Pasteur made his last scientific report in 1888. He intensely regretted no longer being able to do his own research. During his career, he filled one hundred and two laboratory notebooks with an estimated ten thousand pages of cramped writing and illustrations. When

Louis and Marie Pasteur in 1884. *(Courtesy of Musée Pasteur, Paris.)*

told he worked too hard, he replied, "It would seem to me that I was committing a theft if I were to let one day go by without doing some work."

Pasteur spent time visiting rabies victims, especially those who were children. He said: "When I approach a child, he inspires me with two sentiments; that of tenderness for what he is now, and respect for what he may hereafter become." In these young faces he saw the visages of his three dead children, and in the Institute he saw the key to ending the diseases that had plagued him and his family for so long.

Pasteur attended public functions whenever his health allowed. He appeared at the opening ceremony of the new Sorbonne with its beautiful laboratories—a far cry from the dingy labs of the past. Despite his physical condition, when invited to Alès to witness the unveiling of a statue to honor his dead master, Jean-Baptiste

Pasteur's seventieth birthday celebration at the Sorbonne, as depicted in a painting by Rixens. Joseph Lister can be seen approaching Pasteur with open arms. *(Courtesy of Musée Pasteur, Paris.)*

Dumas, Pasteur accepted the invitation, saying, "I am alive; I shall go."

In 1892, a large celebration was held at the Sorbonne to honor Pasteur on his seventieth birthday. The president of France escorted him in, while a government band played a triumphal march. Pasteur was greeted with a resounding ovation. From a small table on stage, he listened to speeches by scientists and dignitaries from around the globe.

When Joseph Lister rose to speak, Pasteur, in a rare display of physical affection, embraced him. Lister gave homage to Pasteur as the man who opened the door to Lister's own antiseptic developments, saying, "You have raised the veil which for centuries had covered infectious diseases...Truly there does not exist in the whole world a person to whom medical science owes more than to you."

The people of Dôle also spoke at his birthday celebration. Pasteur shielded his face to hide the emotion evoked by memories of his parents and of his origin in the tiny village. He knew how significant something tiny could be. They gave him a photograph of the house where he was born, and a reproduction of his birth certificate bearing his father's signature.

Jean-Baptiste once again delivered his father's words to the audience gathered in his honor, expressing Pasteur's hope and belief "that Science and Peace will triumph over Ignorance and War, that nations will unite, not to destroy, but to build, and that the future will belong to those who will have done most for suffering humanity...." Pasteur's speech ended by encouraging the students in the audience to remain determined in their pursuit of knowledge "until the moment when you may experience the supreme happiness of thinking that you have in some way contributed to the progress and the good of humanity. But to whatever degree life will have favored your efforts, when you approach the great goal, you must be able to say to yourself: 'I have done my best.'" At the end of his speech, shouts of "Vive Pasteur!" echoed from the ceiling of the amphitheater.

Pasteur's youthful drive and dedication hardly mellowed with age. He was anxious to be up to date on scientific advances and spent hours talking with the young scientists at the Institute. As always, Marie remained Pasteur's most constant companion and, as his health deteriorated, he came to rely on her even more. Marie had given her life to Pasteur and his work, and was

The last photograph of Louis Pasteur, taken in the garden of the Pasteur Institute in 1895. *(Courtesy of Musée Pasteur, Paris.)*

faithful to him until the end. Albert Calmette, a bacteriologist and future Nobel Prize winner who came to work at the Pasteur Institute, said: "Madame Pasteur, a true scholar's wife, was interested in everything and knew what everyone was thinking and feeling even before they had expressed it. She saw to it with touching solicitude that no worries and preoccupations darkened the meditations and the dreams pursued with such enthusiasm and confidence by those who worked there...."

In November 1894, a month after returning from his last summer in Arbois, Pasteur's kidneys began to fail. His children moved in, taking shifts caring for him. He improved temporarily, and on the one-hundredth anniversary of the École Normale, he invited present and former students into his home. At the gathering, Pasteur expressed regret that he couldn't continue the research he had begun on crystals so many years ago. Roux surprised him with a display of the apparatus from his many experiments. When he saw the display, he clasped Roux's hand and said, "There is still a great deal to do!"

Pasteur was soon confined to his bedroom, where his family read to him of Napoleon's last battles and scenes from the life of St. Vincent de Paul, a peasant's son who devoted his life to helping the poor. As he became weaker, Pasteur knew death was near. When Marie tried to give him a drink of milk, he uttered his last words. Stubborn to the end, he said, "I cannot." Pasteur died around 4:30 p.m. on September 28, 1895, one hand lying in Marie's and the other holding a crucifix. His will was simple: "This is my testament. I leave to my wife as much as I am allowed to leave her under the law. May my children never stray from their duty and continue to give their mother the tenderness she deserves. L. Pasteur."

The funeral procession from the Pasteur Institute to the Notre Dame Cathedral was immense, and was attended by the President of France and all the cabinet ministers, the Grand Duke Constantine of Russia, and Prince Nicholas of Greece. Soldiers surrounded the hearse, and thousands of people came out to pay their respects. Pasteur's name was given to a town in Algeria, a county in Quebec, and streets around the world. He died a national hero. Fittingly, Louis Pasteur was buried under the laboratories of the Pasteur Institute. During World War II, when German troops occupied Paris, Pasteur's most famous patient, Joseph Meister, guarded his tomb. To Meister and countless people who have benefited from his work, Pasteur will always be remembered as a hero. He brought science and medicine closer than ever before. He inaugurated the fields of immunology and microbiology. He made hospitals safer by

Pasteur's grand funeral procession through the Paris streets. *(Courtesy of Musée Pasteur, Paris.)*

Louis Pasteur's ornate mausoleum is located at the Pasteur Institute. *(Courtesy of Musée Pasteur, Paris.)*

urging sanitation, and proved that deadly contagious diseases such as cholera, rabies, and anthrax could be prevented.

Perhaps Pasteur's greatest legacy is in the field of public health. His research revolutionized the prevention and treatment of disease, and life expectancy has risen drastically in the past century, largely as a result of our understanding of germs and how they are transmitted. The impact of many infectious diseases has been greatly reduced through sanitation practices and the widespread availability of vaccines. These improvements would not have been possible without the breakthroughs that Pasteur's research achieved.

Pasteur's discoveries came with a price, however. Marie Pasteur belongs to a long line of women who sacrificed their own desires in order to support their husbands' work. Many others, including laboratory assistants, farm workers, and animal caretakers, helped to make Pasteur's research possible, yet received little or no credit for their contributions. High-level assistants such as Émile Roux clearly deserved greater recognition.

As Pasteur's work continues today, so do the controversies of his time. The hierarchy of the scientific community has come under scrutiny. The use of assistants and, now, graduate students is seen by some as exploitative. The debate over whether to experiment on animals has not been settled. Some people believe vaccines are necessary for all children while others argue that the problems outweigh the benefits. Scientists and laypersons often disagree as to how the scientific community should be held accountable for its work. Although we have established bureaucratic organizations to regulate science, we cannot agree about how much oversight is appropriate.

Louis Pasteur may have been ruthless in his desire for fame, but he was also driven by the desire to save living creatures from disease, and this urge greatly shaped the course of his research. He was dedicated to his science and left his mark on our world. Based on techniques Pasteur developed, researchers at the institute that bears his name still work to find new vaccines, treatments, and cures. The Pasteur Institute and research labs around the world continue to search for ways to use science, as Pasteur did, to save lives.

SOURCES

CHAPTER ONE: "A Dangerous Decision"

p. 11, "Severely bitten on the..." Patrice Debré, *Louis Pasteur* (Paris: Flammarion, 1994), trans. Elborg Forster, (Baltimore: The Johns Hopkins University Press, 1998), 438.

p. 14, "This will be another bad night..." Ibid., 440.

p. 18, "He wasn't a rogue..." Adrien Loir, *A l'Ombre de Pasteur* (Le Mouvement sanitaire,1938), 61.

p. 20, "If I could only get a whiff..." René Vallery-Radot, *The Life of Pasteur,* trans. R.L. Devonshire, (New York: Dover Publications, Inc., 1960), 11-12.

p. 20, "How endless unto watchful anguish..." Ibid., 11.

p. 22, "You remember those days..." Debré, *Louis Pasteur,* 16.

p. 22, "...will power opens the doors..." Ibid., 18.

p. 23, "Once one is used to working..." Ibid., 1.

p. 24, "How often have I cursed..." Ibid., 19.

p. 24, "...I advised you to go..." in Vallery-Radot, *The Life of Pasteur,* 20.

p. 24, "a hundred times..." Debré, *Louis Pasteur,* 20.

p. 25, "Whom do I frequent..." Ibid., 22.

p. 26, "When one wishes..." Vallery-Radot, *The Life of Pasteur,* 22.

p. 26, "Come! Drive out..." Loir, *A l'Ombre de Pasteur,* 60.

CHAPTER TWO: "Emerging Scientist"

p. 27, "You work immoderately..." Pasteur Vallery-Radot, *Louis Pasteur: A Great Life in Brief* (New York: Alfred A. Knopf, Inc., 1958), 25.

p. 27, "You will see what Pasteur..." Vallery-Radot, *The Life of Pasteur,* 32.

p. 29, "For an instant my heart..." René Dubos, *Pasteur: Free Lance of Science* (New York: Charles Scribner's Sons, 1976), 96.

p. 32, "My dear boy, I have loved science..." Debré, *Louis Pasteur,* 48.

p. 35, "I am afraid that Mlle. Marie..." Vallery-Radot, *The Life of Pasteur,* 49.

p. 35, "All that I beg of you..." Ibid., 49.

p. 35, "I woke up every morning..." Beverly Birch, *Louis Pasteur* (Milwaukee: Gareth Stevens, Inc., 1989), 23.

p. 36, "I am often scolded..." Debré, *Louis Pasteur,* 57.

p. 39, "My love to you..." Ibid., 65.

p. 39, "I understand you..." Ibid., 75.

CHAPTER THREE: "Fermentation"

p. 42, "There is no such thing..." Debré, *Louis Pasteur,* 84.

p. 44, "Let us all work..." Ibid., 86.

p. 44, "I will work off the rage..." Vallery-Radot, *The Life of Pasteur,* 423.

p. 46, "I cannot keep my thoughts..." Ibid., 86.

p. 46, "I heard the sound of the coffin..." Debré, *Louis Pasteur,* 124.

CHAPTER FOUR: "Pasteurization"

p. 47, "...these mysterious agents..." Debré, *Louis Pasteur,* 148.

p. 49, "I hope to make soon..." Samuel J. Holmes, *Louis Pasteur* (New York: Dover Publications, Inc., 1924, 1961), 51.

p. 51, "I have taken my drop..." Birch, *Louis Pasteur,* 10.

p. 51, "This is not a matter of religion..." Ibid., 37.

p. 52, "In that case, the air..." Debré, *Louis Pasteur,* 163.

p. 54, "If you understand the question..." Ibid., 128.

p. 58, "I begin to show their majesties..." Ibid., 225.

CHAPTER FIVE: "Saving Silkworms"

p. 63, "Misery is greater here..." Debré, *Louis Pasteur,* 179.

p. 63, "So much the better..." Laura Wood, *Louis Pasteur* (New York: Julian Messner, 1948), 89.

p. 66, "My poor child died..." Debré, *Louis Pasteur,* 124.

p. 69, "There is in my laboratory..." Dubos, *Louis Pasteur,* 218.

p. 72, "In a brood of a hundred..." Vallery-Radot, *The Life of Pasteur,* 139.

p. 73, "Nothing is accomplished..." Émile Duclaux, *Pasteur: The History of a Mind,* (Philadelphia: W.B. Saunders & Company, 1920), 218.

p. 73, "If he was a discoverer..." Émile Duclaux, "Discours aux étudiants de Paris,"18 June, 1896.

p. 73, "But, monsieur, what if there are..." Duclaux, *Pasteur,* 174-175.

p. 75, "Speech clearer..." Vallery-Radot, *The Life of Pasteur,* 160.

p. 75, "Mental faculties still absolutely intact..." Ibid., 160.

p. 76, "I became his tool..." Loir, *A l'Ombre de Pasteur,* 11.

p. 77, "Could Pasteur really have collaborators?..." Debré, *Louis Pasteur,* 141.

p. 78, "I am alive..." Ibid., 216.

CHAPTER SIX: "Anthrax"

p. 80, "I have only one way..." Debré, *Louis Pasteur,* 243.

p. 82, "I would feel as if I had committed..." Vallery-Radot, *Louis Pasteur,* 116.

p. 82, "Now the sight of that parchment..." Vallery-Radot, *The Life of Pasteur,* 190.

p. 83, "Every one of my future works…" Wood, *Louis Pasteur,* 118.

CHAPTER SEVEN: "Vaccines!"
p. 89, "How I wish I had enough health…" Vallery-Radot, *The Life of Pasteur,* 232.
p. 90, "I shall force them…" Ibid., 292.
p. 92, "A pin-prick…" Ibid., 234.
p. 93, "medical doctrine which I believe…" Ibid., 256.
p. 93, "None of those things cause…" Ibid., 291.
p. 94, "No one knows what feelings…" Ibid., 289.
p. 98, "If it is terrifying to think…" Ibid., 272.
p. 100, "Microbiolatry is the fashion…" Ibid., 313-314.
p. 101, "stunning success" Ibid., 322.
p. 102, "Here it is! Oh ye…" Debré, *Louis Pasteur,* 400.
p. 102, "Long live Pasteur!…" Vallery-Radot, *The Life of Pasteur,* 373.
p. 103, "My dear Pasteur, forty years ago…" Ibid., 354-355.
p. 104, "The discoveries of bacteria are among…" Debré, *Louis Pasteur,* 411.
p. 104, "…it would be really beautiful…" Vallery-Radot, *The Life of Pasteur,* 340.
p. 105, "The most striking thing…" in Debré, *Louis Pasteur,* 375.
p. 105, "In each one of us there are two men…" Dubos, *Louis Pasteur,* 390-391.
p. 106, "Let me tell you the secret…" in Birch, *Louis Pasteur,* 6.
p. 106, "Your father is as preoccupied…" Vallery-Radot, *The Life of Pasteur,* 396.

CHAPTER EIGHT: "The Invisible Virus"
p. 113, "I have not yet dared…" Debré, *Louis Pasteur,* 428.

p. 113, "Even when I have multiplied examples…" Holmes, *Louis Pasteur,* 127.

p. 118, "Among the great men…" Debré, *Louis Pasteur,* 445.

p. 120, "Pasteur's work is admirable…" Vallery-Radot, *Louis Pasteur,* 86.

p. 120, "He does not cure individuals…" Vallery-Radot, *The Life of Pasteur,* 383.

p. 122, "Always cultivate the spirit of criticism…" Debre, *Louis Pasteur,* 472.

CHAPTER NINE: "Pasteur Passes On"

p. 124, "It would seem to me that I was committing…" Vallery-Radot, *The Life of Pasteur,* 363.

p. 124, "When I see a child…" Ibid., 447.

p. 125, "I am alive…" Ibid., 446.

p. 125, "You have raised the veil…" LisaYount, *The Importance of Louis Pasteur* (San Diego: Lucent Books,1994), 78.

p. 126, "that Science and Peace will triumph…" Vallery-Radot, *The Life of Pasteur,* 450-451.

p. 126, "until the moment…" Debré, *Louis Pasteur,* 493.

p. 127, "Madame Pasteur, a true scholar's wife…" Debré, *Louis Pasteur,* 483-484.

p. 128, "There is still a great deal…" Vallery-Radot, *The Life of Pasteur,* 461.

p. 128, "I cannot." Ibid., 464.

p. 128, "This is my testament…" Debré, *Louis Pasteur,* 496.

BIBLIOGRAPHY

Birch, Beverly. *Louis Pasteur.* Milwaukee: Gareth Stevens Children's Books, 1989.

Bynum, W. F. "The Scientist As Antihero." *Nature,* Vol. 375, 4 May 1995.

Debré, Patrice. *Louis Pasteur.* Paris: Flammarion, 1994. English translation: Baltimore: The Johns Hopkins University Press, 1998.

Dubos, René. *Louis Pasteur: Free Lance of Science.* Boston: Little, Brown and Company, 1950.

———. *Pasteur: Free Lance of Science.* New York: Charles Scribner's Sons, 1976.

Duclaux, Émile. "Discours aux étudiants de Paris." 1896.

———. *Pasteur: The History of a Mind.* Philadelphia: W.B. Saunders & Company, 1920.

Geison, Gerald L. *The Private Science of Pasteur.* Princeton: Princeton University Press, 1995.

Holmes, Samuel J. *Louis Pasteur.* New York: Dover Publications, Inc., 1961.

Loir, Adrien. *A l'Ombre de Pasteur.* Le Mouvement sanitaire, 1938.

Mann, John. *Pasteur: Founder of Bacteriology.* New York: Charles Scribner's Sons, 1964.

Metchnikoff, Elie. *The Founders of Modern Medicine: Pasteur, Koch, Lister.* New York: Walden Publications, 1939.

Morgan, Nina. *Pasteur.* New York: The Bookwright Press, 1992.

Newfield, Marcia. *The Life of Louis Pasteur.* Pioneers in Health and Medicine. Frederick, Maryland: Twenty-First Century Books, A Division of Henry Holt and Co., Inc., 1992.

Nicolle, Jacques. *Louis Pasteur: The Story of His Major Discoveries.* New York: Basic Books, 1961.

Paget, Stephen. "The Spectator." 1 October 1910, pp. 509-510.

Perutz, M. F. "The Pioneer Defended." *The New York Review,* 21 December 1995.

Porter, J. R. "Pasteur Sesquicentennial (1822-1972)." *Science,* 22 December, 1972.

Reynolds, Moira Davison. *How Pasteur Changed History.* Bradenton, Florida: McGuinn & McGuire Publishing, Inc., 1994.

Vallery-Radot, Pasteur. *Louis Pasteur: A Great Life in Brief.* New York: Alfred A. Knopf, Inc., 1958.

Vallery-Radot, René *The Life of Pasteur.* New York: Dover Publications, Inc., 1960.

———. *Madame Pasteur.* Paris: Ernest Flammarion, 1941.

Williams-Ellis, Amabel. *They Wanted the Real Answers.* New York: C.P. Putnam & Sons, 1958.

Wood, Laura N. *Louis Pasteur.* New York: Julian Messner, 1948.

Yount, Lisa. *The Importance of Louis Pasteur.* San Diego: Lucent Books,1994.

WEBSITES

Institut Pasteur
http://www.pasteur.fr/english.html

Le Musée Pasteur, Dole (click on British flag for English translation of site)
http://www.musee-pasteur.com/

Science World: Wolfram Research
http://scienceworld.wolfram.com/biography/Pasteur.html

The Life and Times of Louis Pasteur by David V. Cohn, Ph.D.
http://www.labexplorer.com/louis_pasteur.htm

INDEX